STRATEGIC DISCIPLE MAKING

A PRACTICAL TOOL
for SUCCESSFUL MINISTRY

AUBREY MALPHURS

BakerBooks

a division of Baker Publishing Group
Grand Rapids, Michigan

© 2009 by Aubrey Malphurs

Published by Baker Books
a division of Baker Publishing Group
P.O. Box 6287, Grand Rapids, MI 49516-6287
www.bakerbooks.com

Printed in the United States of America

All rights reserved. No part of this publication may be reproduced, stored in a retrieval system, or transmitted in any form or by any means—for example, electronic, photocopy, recording—without the prior written permission of the publisher. The only exception is brief quotations in printed reviews.

Library of Congress Cataloging-in-Publication Data
Malphurs, Aubrey.
    Strategic disciple making : a practical tool for successful ministry / Aubrey Malphurs.
        p.   cm.
    Includes bibliographical references and index.
    ISBN 978-0-8010-9196-4 (pbk.)
    1. Discipling (Christianity) I. Title.
BV4520.M34 2009
253—dc22   2008038690

Unless otherwise indicated, Scripture is taken from the HOLY BIBLE, NEW INTERNATIONAL VERSION®. NIV®. Copyright © 1973, 1978, 1984 by International Bible Society. Used by permission of Zondervan. All rights reserved.

In keeping with biblical principles of creation stewardship, Baker Publishing Group advocates the responsible use of our natural resources. As a member of the Green Press Initiative, our company uses recycled paper when possible. The text paper of this book is comprised of 30% post-consumer waste.

green
press
INITIATIVE

CONTENTS

120332

INTRODUCTION

Why have I written this book? What were the seeds that germinated this plant? It began with my passion for the Great Commission, specifically Matthew 28:19–20 where Jesus says to the Twelve, "Make disciples!" This is Jesus's marching orders for his church. Most would agree that this is one passage of several that addresses the mission of the church. But what does it mean? To take seriously and obey Christ's command to make disciples, we must understand what it means or we're flying in the dark. Churches that don't understand Matthew's version of Jesus's Great Commission are much like an oceangoing vessel that is plowing through fog-enshrouded, iceberg-infested waters without navigation equipment.

For much of my life as a Christian, I have either attended or pastored what is known in some areas of the country as a Bible church. And most traditional Bible churches have interpreted Matthew 28:19–20 to mean that the church's mission is to teach the Bible—to make disciples simply means to teach people the Bible. I was told, "If you preach and teach the Bible, everything else will fall into place." But this has not proved true.

So what does the Great Commission mean? The real problem in the Matthew passage is the term *disciple*. What is a disciple? Ask most Christians who regularly attend a church, or even a class of seminary students who are preparing to be pastors, and you'll get a variety of answers. By the way, how would you answer the question?

While my passion for Jesus's Great Commission motivated the writing of this work, God used a recent experience to urge me to do it now. One of my fellow faculty members at Dallas Seminary who teaches a class on biblical discipleship was out of town. Rather than cancel the class, he invited two other people and me, knowing of my interest in the topic, to address his class. One of the other speakers was a young man who was involved in discipling several committed men in his church. The other was a local pastor's wife who had a passion for discipling some of the women in her church.

I was excited about the opportunity and presented first. The content consisted mostly of the material in this book, shoehorned into a five-minute presentation. When I sat down, I noticed that the man and woman were not smiling and both were staring at the floor to avoid eye contact with me. After I heard their presentations, I understood why. Our views of discipleship were polar opposites.

A Quiz

Before you read any further, take the following quiz and see how you do. Determine whether the following six statements are true or false.

1. The only way to disciple a person is for a gifted, mature Christian to work one-on-one with a believer who desires to grow in Christ.
2. A disciple is a Christian, but a Christian may not be a disciple.
3. Discipleship is only one of several key ministries in the church.
4. The church should focus primarily on discipling those who are serious about Christianity.
5. Discipleship involves the edification of the saints not the evangelism of sinners.
6. Discipleship is best accomplished by a few in the church who are trained to disciple those who are serious about their commitment to Christ.

The answer to all the above questions is false.

So how did you do? Have I piqued your curiosity? Have I upset you? Perhaps you're shaking your head in disagreement. Or maybe you're nodding your head in agreement. Regardless of your response, read on!

The Question

Whether or not you concur with my answers to the quiz, I'm sure you would agree that every church should have a simple, clear pathway for making authentic disciples. So the question is, Does your church have such a strategy in place? Does it have a game plan for making disciples? If a new Christian visited your church and asked you or someone in the church how you would help him or her to grow as one of Christ's disciples, what would your answer be? What would be the first step? And what would be the second? My experience is that most churches either wouldn't have an answer or wouldn't have a clear answer, because most church leaders simply aren't thinking that way. I'm convinced, however, that such a response can change so that our churches have a biblical, Christ-honoring answer and thus have a greater impact in the twenty-first century.

This Book Is for You!

I wrote this book for anyone in Christ's church who takes seriously Christ's Great Commission to make disciples. This would include senior pastors, pastors of small churches, executive pastors, other church staff, governing boards, congregants, consultants, professors, and denominational executives. I believe that all are responsible for being a part of the discipleship process if a church is going to obey the Savior. The church's success depends on those who own and implement Jesus's mission for our church.

Where Am I Going?

I have divided this book into two parts. Part 1 *prepares* the reader for making mature disciples and prepares the way for part 2. Part 1 addresses the church's disciple-making mission, the current state of church discipleship, and the definitions of *disciple* and *discipleship*; it asks who is responsible for making disciples in the church; it presents Jesus's message and methods for making disciples; and it covers the church's message and methods for making disciples in the first century. Part 2 *presents* the process for making mature disciples. Using a tool I call the Maturity Matrix, it addresses the characteristics of a mature disciple, the ministries for making disciples, how to measure the church's disciple-making efforts, and how to use the Maturity Matrix to recruit staff and develop the budget.

The Value of the Maturity Matrix

There are five ways that the matrix will have value for you and your church.

1. Most importantly, it will guide you as you design a simple, clear strategy, process, or pathway for developing authentic disciples in your church.
2. It will help you understand your current process for making or attempting to make disciples.
3. It will enable you to analyze, critique, and recritique your process. What are its strengths and weaknesses? What is sound and what needs to be shored up?
4. It will assist you in developing your disciple-making process. You will address the question: Now that we have critiqued our process, how can we as a church improve our disciple making?
5. It will enable you to understand other churches' disciple-making processes. You can place what they are doing on the matrix, and it will help you analyze and comprehend their processes. Often an understanding of other processes will aid you in improving your own process.

The Context

One of the first principles of good Bible study is to interpret a biblical passage in its context. This principle teaches that context is important. That is true for any topic, including this book. So what's the context for this book? It is strategic envisioning (planning). I argue that the way a church makes disciples is vital to how it does strategic planning. I wrote *Advanced Strategic Planning*[1] to help churches in general and their leaders in particular think and act strategically. This does not involve mimicking some church model, which seldom works, but working one's way through Christ's church-building process (see Matt. 16:18), which consists of touching four bases.

The first base is to discover the ministry's core values so that it knows why it does what it does or does not do what it should do (such as make disciples). Core values get at the church's DNA or core identity. The second and third bases are the church's mission and vision, both of which help the church discover and articulate its direction—making mature disciples. The last base is the church's strategy, which enables it to accomplish its mission and vision. It is made up of five key elements.

1. The church's *strategy for discovering its community*—its future disciples.
2. The church's *strategy for making and maturing disciples*. Once the church knows who makes up its community, it must determine what it plans to do for that community. The answer is to design a strategic process—detailed in this book—to help the people become disciples or believers and, in time, mature disciples.
3. The church's *team strategy*, which asks, Who is the disciple-making team?
4. The *strategy for its location and facilities*, which asks, Where can we best make disciples?
5. A *stewardship strategy*, which addresses how the church will raise the funds necessary for the disciple-making process.

Further Help

Finally, there are questions at the end of each chapter. They are designed to help you reflect on the chapter's contents. I encourage you to read this book with others in your church and use these questions to provoke discussion about your church and how it makes disciples. If you are a pastor, I encourage you to read this book with your board and/or staff.

PART 1

THE PREPARATION
for MAKING MATURE DISCIPLES

The purpose of this book is to help you and your church obey Jesus's command in Matthew 28:19 to make disciples. We will better accomplish this if we clearly understand what the Bible teaches about disciples and how to make them. This part of the book will address a number of introductory issues, such as the church's biblical mission, how well churches are accomplishing this mission, and the definitions of *disciple* and *disciple making*. The main thrust of this part is to address Jesus's message and methods for making disciples, found in the Gospels, and the church's message and methods, found in the book of Acts and in the Epistles. We want to discover the similarities and differences in the messages and methods that were used.

1

WHAT ARE WE
SUPPOSED TO BE DOING?

The Church's Mission

The question in the title of this chapter points us to the biblical mission of Christ's church on earth. Before I address this question, however, I believe it is important to first address what churches *are* doing.

What Are We Doing?

Perhaps the most important questions that the church and its leadership can ask are, What does God want us to do? What is our mission? What are our marching orders? The answers are not hard to find. More than two thousand years ago, the Savior predetermined the church's mission. It's the Great Commission, as found in such texts as Matthew 28:19–20; Mark 16:15; Luke 24:46–49; John 20:21; and Acts 1:8.

The Great Commission Passages

Matthew 28:19–20
Mark 16:15
Luke 24:46–49
John 20:21
Acts 1:8

As I consult with churches and research churches from border to border and coast to coast, I find that most are not following Christ's command in Matthew 28:19–20 to make disciples. While all churches have a mission, the mission is not necessarily Christ's mission.

I used to tell churches without a Great Commission mission that they do not have a mission and need to develop one. I have since changed my mind. Every church has a set of core values, and those values drive the church toward and cause it to establish its mission. For example, the church may have a strong Bible teaching ministry because it values the Scriptures highly. Thus its sole mission, whether held at a conscious or, more likely, an unconscious level, is to communicate the Scriptures. Though this is a worthy endeavor, it is not the church's Great Commission mission. Below I discuss several missions of the church that have developed because of the specific value or values of individual churches.

Caring for People

My experience is that the majority of smaller churches in North America, especially those populated mainly by the Builder generation, believe the church's sole mission and the primary role of the pastor is to take care of its people. This is true especially of those living in more rural areas of the country. This hands-on care involves such services as home and hospital visitation as well as crisis counseling. Should a new, inexperienced pastor not be aware of these expectations and fail to visit Grandma or Grandpa in the hospital, he will discover that he has likely offended not only Grandma or Grandpa but the entire family. Should he not correct this major faux pas, many in the congregation will assume he doesn't like them and wonder what is wrong with him and why he is in ministry.

Where did the Builder generation get this idea? There are two sources. One is a misunderstanding of the biblical use of the shepherd imagery. Many assume that in the first century shepherds mostly took care of sheep. While shepherds did take care of sheep, they did much more than that. They were more than pastoral caregivers, they were pastoral leaders as well. In addition to this misunderstanding, in the 1600s the Puritans stressed that the pastor is a "physician of the soul." Specifically they stressed the importance that he be a pastoral caregiver more than a congregational leader. (For more on pastoral care and the role of the pastor, see appendix A.)

Teaching the Bible

Often an unstated mission of churches, especially those in the Bible church movement (my roots), is to teach people the Bible. In these churches, the primary expectation of the pastor is to teach the Bible well and with some depth. Thus he may spend all week in the study, preparing for Sunday's sermon. I find that many evangelical seminaries and Bible colleges hold this view concerning the mission of the church. In a church with this mission, if the pastor is not a good Bible teacher or places the emphasis somewhere else, he may not be around for very long. People will become dissatisfied and wonder why he isn't teaching the Bible.

Where did this view come from? While the mission of caring for people came down to us from the Puritan tradition, this view came down as a part of the tradition of the Reformers. During the Reformation, the Reformers emphasized the teaching of the Scriptures. Prior to this time in church history, the Roman Catholic Church taught little Bible from the pulpit and even discouraged doing it.

Evangelizing Lost People

An unstated mission in some churches is to win lost people to faith in Christ. This used to be the predominant mission of many churches in the first half of the twentieth century, especially Baptist churches. In the late twentieth and early twenty-first century, I have detected a move away from this mission. Few churches seem to value evangelism, and not much of it is taking place as it was earlier. In fact, evangelism seems to be a dying value in far too many churches in the twenty-first century. While evangelism isn't the church's sole mission, it is a part of its mission.

Worshiping God

Some churches believe that their mission is to worship God. They have caught the importance of worship and emphasize it above all else. Often this is the case in classical and liturgical churches, and they reflect this emphasis in the mission statement. However, I would argue from a theological perspective that the church's worship of God is one of five functions of the church (worship, fellowship, biblical instruction, evangelism, and service) that come under the church's mission. But worship is *not* the church's sole mission.

Ministering to Families

I am aware of at least one church that believes its mission is to help parents minister to their family. The pastor and the church highly value family. It is the church's overarching primary value that influences its other values and all its ministries. People go to this church because of the help it provides in growing strong, biblically focused families. While no one would object to this as a core value in the church, we must object to its being the mission of the church. Again, the church's overall mission is to make disciples, not only to focus on and help its families. I would argue that ministering to families is a part of discipleship, but this involves more than just ministering to adults and their children.

Church Missions

Driving Values	Resulting Missions
Pastoral Care	Caring for people
Scripture	Teaching the Bible
Evangelism	Evangelizing lost people
Worship	Worshiping God
Family	Ministering to families

What Are We Supposed to Be Doing?

The sampling of wrong missions above helps us better understand that the church's true mission is the Great Commission. You may wonder how I know this and what the Great Commission really is. My hope is that, as we look closely at Matthew 28:19–20, this will become clear.

The Church's Mission

Most scholars would agree that the church's mission is the Great Commission, found in Matthew 28:19–20; Mark 16:15; Luke 24:46–49; John 20:21; and Acts 1:8. It makes sense that as Jesus prepared to leave this earth, he provided his disciples (the apostles) with their life's mission. And his last words are lasting words. Several times I have come across Christians who have argued that the Great Commission was given solely to the disciples, not to the church. Thus, they say, it is not the church's commission but only the disciples' commission. This is a poor argument. The book of Acts makes it very clear that the disciples took on the primary leadership role in the early church as apostles (they are called apostles only in Acts to emphasize their new role). And their mission, in turn, becomes the church's mission. While they were apostles, they were still disciples as well and represented all Christ's disciples. Thus what he gave to them as his disciples, he gives to all his disciples.

Understanding the Great Commission

What exactly is the Great Commission? To answer this question, I have placed the Great Commission passages in the chart below, identifying each passage in the first column. The subsequent columns indicate those to whom the Savior addressed the message, what he said (the essence of the commission), those to whom the commission was given, how they were to do what

Christ commanded them, and where it was to take place. I've not included John 20:21 here because it addresses only the sending of the disciples.

Scripture	Who	What	To Whom	How	Where
Matthew 28:19–20	Disciples	"Go and make disciples."	All nations	Baptizing and teaching	
Mark 16:15	Disciples	"Go . . . and preach the good news."	All creation		All the world
Luke 24:46–49	Disciples	"[Be] witnesses."	All nations	Preaching repentance and forgiveness of sins	Beginning in Jerusalem
Acts 1:8	Disciples	"Be my witnesses."		With power	Jerusalem, Judea, Samaria, the whole earth

We can make seven observations about the Great Commission:

1. Each passage is addressed to the disciples as the future apostles and leaders of the church.
2. All the passages are imperatives that spell out Christ's mandate for his church.
3. All the verses emphasize evangelism: "Be witnesses," "Preach the good news," and so on.
4. Both Matthew 28:19–20 and Mark 16:15 command the disciples to go, not retreat. Thus the Great Commission is a proactive not a passive venture. Whereas far too many North American churches are waiting for people to come to them (their ministries are "attractional" or invitational, not missional or incarnational), the Great Commission commands that we go to the people.
5. They were to go to "all nations," not just Israel. In the Great Commission, Christ has included both Israel and the Gentiles.
6. Putting the verses together, we find that the church is to preach repentance and the forgiveness of sins and then baptize and teach those who respond. And this is to be done in the power of the Holy Spirit.
7. There are to be no geographical limitations. The whole world is the church's mission field. And Acts 1:8 would seem to have geographical and ethnological implications. Each church is to reach out to its Jerusalem, its Judea and Samaria, and to the ends of the earth. They are to disciple those in each church's community as well as on the international mission field. Note that Christ included the Samaritans, who were not

Jews. The implication is that we are to go to those who are ethnically different from us.

Understanding Matthew 28:19–20

Some people question whether Matthew 28:19–20 clearly teaches that the church is to do evangelism. Matthew teaches this, but perhaps it is not clear to the twenty-first-century reader. The problem and question here is, What did Jesus mean when he commanded his church to make disciples? Is this passage talking about evangelism, or is it talking about growing believers up in their faith, or could it be both?

Should you ask ten different people in the church (including the pastoral staff) what a disciple is, you might get ten different answers. The same is true at a seminary. If the church is not clear on what Jesus meant, then it will be difficult to comply with his expressed will. For the church to understand what the Savior meant in Matthew 28:19–20, we must examine the main imperative: "make disciples." What did Jesus mean?

A common view is that a disciple is a committed believer. Thus a disciple is a believer, but a believer isn't necessarily a disciple. But that's not how the New Testament uses this term. I contend that the normative use of the term *disciple* is for one who is a convert to or a believer in Jesus Christ (there are a few exceptions to this—"the disciples of Moses" in John 9:28 and the "disciples" of the Pharisees in Matt. 22:16, for example). Thus the Bible teaches that a disciple is not necessarily a Christian who has made a deeper commitment to the Savior but simply a Christian. Committed Christians are committed disciples. Uncommitted Christians are uncommitted disciples. This is clearly how Luke uses the term *disciple* in the book of Acts and his Gospel. It is evident in passages such as the following: Acts 6:1–2, 7; 9:1, 26; 11:26; 14:21–22; 15:10; 18:23; 19:9. A great example is Acts 14:21, where Luke says they made "disciples" in connection with evangelism. Here they preached the gospel and won or made a large number of disciples or converts, not mature or even growing Christians. Disciples, then, were synonymous with believers. Virtually all scholars acknowledge this to be the case in Acts.

However, we must not stop here. Much of Jesus's teaching of the Twelve (who are believers, except for Judas) concerns the need for the disciple to grow in Christ (see Matt. 16:24–26 and Luke 9:23–25). For example, Matthew 16:24 says, "Then Jesus said to his disciples, 'If anyone would come after me, he must deny himself and take up his cross and follow me.'"

So how does this relate to the passages in Acts and the other commission passages in the Gospels? The answer is that the Great Commission has both an evangelism and an edification or spiritual growth component. To make a disciple, first one has to win a person (a nondisciple) to Christ. At that point he or she becomes a disciple. It doesn't stop there. Now the new disciple needs to grow or mature as a disciple, hence the edification component. While the other Great Commission texts stress evangelism (see my observations above), I believe that the command to "make disciples" in Matthew 28:19 stresses both concepts—evangelism and edification. (There is a more in-depth study of what Jesus meant in Matthew 28:19–20 in appendix B for the reader who wants more detail.)

Jesus was clear about his intentions for his church. It wasn't just to teach or preach the Word, as important as that is. Nor was it evangelism alone, although this is emphasized as much as teaching. He expects his entire church (not simply a few passionate disciple makers) to move people along a maturity or disciple-making continuum from prebirth (unbelief) to the new birth (belief) and then to maturity.

Disciple-Making Continuum

Nondisciple	New Disciple	Growing Disciple
Prebirth (unbelief)	New birth (belief)	Maturity (growth)

In fact, this is so important that we can measure a church's spiritual health and its ultimate success by its obedience to the Great Commission. Therefore, it is fair to ask of every church's ministry how many people have become disciples (believers) and how many of these disciples are growing toward maturity. In short, it's imperative that every church make and mature disciples at home and abroad!

Questions for Reflection and Discussion

1. Does your church have a mission statement? If so, what is it? Does it consist of the Great Commission?
2. If your church doesn't have a mission statement, it still has a mission. Based on its values and what people seem to emphasize and value most, what might that mission be? Is it the Great Commission? If not, is it one of the missions addressed in this chapter, such as to take care of people, and so on?
3. Do you agree that the church's mission is the Great Commission? Why or why not? If it is not the Great Commission, then what is it?
4. What is the Great Commission? How would you define a disciple? Do you agree or disagree with the author's definition? What do you think Jesus meant when he said "make disciples"?

2

HOW ARE WE DOING?

The Current State of Disciple Making

The church's marching orders are very clear. We learned in the last chapter that we are to make disciples. The church is to pursue and make and mature believers at home and abroad. So we must ask, How are we doing? And the answer depends on whom you ask—the average churchgoer, a pollster, or others.

Who Is Making Disciples?

If you were to ask the average person in the American church who is making disciples, he or she would identify his or her church. My experience is that while many realize the church is struggling as of late, they still believe that their church is doing okay. When I think of these people, I picture an ostrich with its head buried in the sand. And when I consult with these churches, the first item on my agenda is to gently pull their heads out of the sand and help them take a look at reality.

How do I accomplish this? What I do with them is what I am about to do with you. I provide them with some information on how the church in America is doing. When I did this in one church several years ago, a male Baby Boomer came up to me afterward and communicated the following simile. He said his church was like an ocean liner floating in iceberg-infested waters, and the leaders could not see the icebergs because there was a heavy fog concealing

them. Then he added that the information I supplied on churches in general and his church in particular blew the fog away to reveal that they were on a collision course with several icebergs.

Western European Churches

I am convinced that, based on what has taken place in Western European churches over the past century, the decline in America's churches could have been predicted. The center of gravity in the Christian world has shifted away from Europe southward to the continents of Asia, Africa, and Latin America. Christianity on these continents is growing, contrary to what many believe.

Author Philip Jenkins writes of Europe: "In 1950, a list of the world's leading Christian countries would have included Britain, France, Spain, and Italy, but none of these names would be represented in a corresponding list for 2050."[1] They have become part of an emerging post-Christian culture. Again Jenkins writes: "Over the past century or so, massive secularization has seriously reduced the population of European Christians. . . . Rates of church membership and religious participation have been declining precipitously in a long-term trend that shows no signs of slowing."[2] Then he cites Great Britain as an example of de-Christianization:

> According to a survey taken in 2000, 44 percent of the British claim no religious affiliation whatever, a number that has grown from 31 percent in 1983. More worrying still for the churches, two-thirds of those ages 18–24 now describe themselves as non-religious: almost half of young adults do not even believe that Jesus existed as a historical person, which is quite a radical stance.[3]

He concludes, "The era of Western Christianity has passed within our lifetimes, and the day of Southern Christianity is dawning."[4]

Why do I even mention the decline that has taken place in the Western European church? Americans must remember that Western Europe was the cradle out of which American Christianity was born. The church in America owes much to its predecessor—the church in Europe. And the question we must ask is, Could the same thing that has taken place in Western Europe happen in America? I think the answer is yes.

American Churches

When we look at how the American church is doing, we realize that the answer is, not well. The church is an organization as well as an organism. Thus,

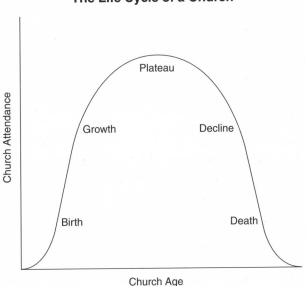

The Life Cycle of a Church

like other organizations, churches experience growth, eventually a plateau, and ultimately decline. I call this the organizational life cycle.

Where is the church in America on the life cycle? As many as 80 to 85 percent if not higher of American churches are plateaued or dying. While a number of church organizations and denominations have returned to church planting, this has not yet stemmed the tide toward a post-Christian culture in the United States.

Along with the plateau and decline of the American church, a significant number of Americans are unchurched. George Gallup defines the unchurched as "those who are not members of a church or have not attended services in the previous six months other than for special religious holidays, weddings, funerals or the like."[5] Christian pollster George Barna writes that the number of unchurched Americans has increased 92 percent in the last thirteen years.[6] And the Barna Group's research shows that, as of March 2005, one-third of all adults, or 34 percent, are unchurched.[7] In one article Barna points out the generational differences in church attendance: 35 percent of Mosaics, 30 percent of Busters, 49 percent of Boomers, and 54 percent of Builders attend church on any given Sunday.[8] The following chart shows how many are unchurched by generation.

Generation	Birth Years	Percentage Unchurched
Builders	1927–1945	46 percent
Boomers	1946–1964	51 percent
Busters	1965–1983	70 percent
Mosaics	1984–2002	65 percent

We must note that the Busters and Mosaics (some refer to these generations as Generation X and Millennials or Generation Y) are essentially unchurched generations (65 to 70 percent). These two younger generations are the future of our churches as well as our nation. Consequently, these statistics cast a dark shadow over the church's future.

As if this information were not bad enough, a number of people challenge the reliability of Barna's statistics. They believe that he is too optimistic. We must understand that the Barna Group and other pollsters such as Gallup gather their information by polling people through self-identification or self-reporting surveys. So we must ask to what degree we should trust these findings.

Pollster Lou Harris concedes, "It should be noted that church attendance is notoriously over-reported as a socially desirable activity, so true attendance figures are surely lower than those reported here."[9] Barry Kosmin, codirector of the 2001 American Religious Identification Survey, notes in USA Today: "Leadership of all faiths exaggerate or manufacture their numbers."[10] And C. Kirk Hadaway and his team of sociologists have challenged the accuracy of the polls. In their article "What the Polls Don't Show," they differed with Gallup's earlier finding that 60 percent of Americans were unchurched. Their research indicated that 80 percent of Protestants and 72 percent of Catholics are unchurched. Their conclusion was that poll respondents in self-reports substantially overstate their church attendance.[11]

David Olson is the director of the American Church Research Project as well as the director of Church Planting for the Evangelical Covenant Church in America. He has collected research information on American churches for the past eighteen years. Using data from the Glenmary Research Center in Cincinnati, Ohio, as well as other sources, he reports the following:

On any given weekend in 1990, 20.4 percent of the American population attended
an orthodox Christian church. On any given weekend in 2000, 18.7 percent of
the American population attended an orthodox Christian church. In 2003 the
Christian church attendance percentage was 17.8 percent. If the present rate of
decline continues, in 2050 11.7 percent of the population will be in a Christian
church on any given weekend.[12]

Finally, he notes that evangelical churches, as opposed to orthodox (mainline)
churches, went from 9.2 percent of the population in attendance in 1990 to
9.0 percent in 2000, a decline of 3 percent.[13]

American Population Attending an Orthodox Christian Church

Year	Percentage
1990	20.4 percent
2000	18.7 percent
2003	17.8 percent
2050	11.7 percent

In 1994 Bob Gilliam, cofounder and president of T-NET International,
developed the "Spiritual Journey Evaluation" as an attempt to determine if
today's church is making disciples. The survey included almost four thousand
attenders in thirty-five churches in several denominations scattered from Florida
to Washington. After analyzing the results, Gilliam observed: "Most people
in these churches are not growing spiritually. Of those taking this survey, 24
percent indicated that their behavior was sliding backward and 41 percent
said they were 'static' in their spiritual growth."[14] Therefore, 65 percent of
those responding indicated that they were either plateaued or declining in
their spiritual growth.

Even some of the premier churches that have had a huge impact for Christ
over the past twenty years acknowledge some struggle. One example is Willow Creek Community Church (located outside Chicago, Illinois). In 2007 the
senior pastor, Bill Hybels, wrote that "nearly one out of every four people
at Willow Creek were stalled in their spiritual growth or dissatisfied with the
church."[15]

Why Is This Important?

The Savior has made it very clear what the church is supposed to do. What
could be more important than making disciples? These survey results are
important for at least two reasons. The first is current: the survey gives us an

idea as to how the church is doing today in its obedience to the Commission. The second is future: the church's capacity to obey Jesus and make disciples will have a direct impact on the future of Christianity in America.

This quote from Dietrich Bonhoeffer sums it up well:

> Christianity without discipleship is always Christianity without Christ. Discipleship means adherence to Christ, and, because Christ is the object of that adherence, it must take the form of discipleship. An abstract Christology, a doctrinal system, a general religious knowledge of the subject of grace or on the forgiveness of sins render discipleship superfluous, and in fact, they positively exclude any idea of discipleship whatever, and are essentially inimical to the whole conception of following Christ. With an abstract idea it is possible to enter into a relation of formal knowledge, to become enthusiastic about it, and perhaps even to put it into practice; but it can never be followed in personal obedience. Christianity without the living Christ is inevitably Christianity without discipleship, and Christianity without discipleship is always Christianity without Christ.[16]

Questions for Reflection and Discussion

1. How is your church doing? Where would you place it on the organizational life cycle? Would others agree with your assessment? Why or why not? How might you use this information to get the attention of those who want to preserve the status quo?

2. If someone asked you whether your church is making disciples, what would your answer be? Why are you or why are you not making disciples?

3. Are the churches in Europe making disciples? What lesson or lessons might we learn from the churches in Europe? Do you believe that they are predictive of where churches in America are headed?

4. Statistics seem to indicate that the churches in America are struggling and that we have a large number of unchurched people in this country. Did this catch you by surprise? Why or why not? How many unchurched people do you believe live in your community? Do you know any of them?

5. Of the number of unchurched people in America, the largest percentage are Busters and Mosaics. Why is this problematic? What might it say about the future of the church? How might this information help you to get the attention of the people in your church who have assumed the "ostrich position"?

3

WHAT ARE WE TALKING ABOUT?

The Definition of Disciple Making

Perhaps you have found yourself in an intense conversation with another person with whom you could not agree on a matter. You may have gone so far as to lose your temper with the person, only to discover that you were not even talking about the same thing. Not only is this embarrassing, but it can leave one feeling a bit silly.

Definitions are important, but how many of us take time to ask another to define his or her terms? For example, *leadership* is a hot topic today with many in the Christian community, yet I have observed that very few people who address this topic pause long enough to define what a leader is. And much of the time I wonder if they are all talking about the same thing. This applies especially to leadership development. How can we know if we are developing leaders if we do not take time to define what a leader is?

In this chapter I will define what disciple making is about in the context of the terms *disciple* and especially *discipleship*. As we have seen in prior chapters, in Matthew 28:19–20 Jesus has given his church instructions on what it is supposed to be doing. There he tells his church to "make disciples." This is what I am referring to when I use the term *disciple making*. And any discussion of disciple making surfaces two key terms—*disciple* and *discipleship*. But what is a disciple, and what is discipleship? What does each term mean, and how do they relate to disciple making? There are far too many divergent answers, and our goal in this chapter is to discover what the terms mean to better get a grasp of disciple making.

First, we will focus on four views or models of disciple making that illustrate what it is not. Then we will explore several definitions that will help us understand what it is.

What Disciple Making Is Not

For years parachurch ministries, such as Campus Crusade for Christ and The Navigators, have been known for their emphasis on discipleship. One of the reasons (often the reason for the founding and existence of parachurch organizations) is the church's failure to make disciples. The founders of parachurch organizations reason that if the church is not going to do what it is supposed to (evangelism, discipleship, leadership development, and so on), then somebody has to do it, and that somebody is "us." In the last twenty or more years, a number of churches have discovered or rediscovered the Great Commission and have made disciples. Along with established and some new parachurch ministries, they have produced a growing literature of discipleship. However, if you explore this material, you will discover a number of different, often conflicting positions on the nature of discipleship.

In his book *Following the Master*, New Testament scholar Michael Wilkins notes this growth and isolates five models or views of discipleship that will help you determine your definitions of a disciple and discipleship.[1] These models are helpful and are similar to the four models I present below. As you read the description of each model and evaluate it, determine which one, if any, best represents your view.

Learners

The first model of discipleship asserts that a disciple is a learner who follows a great teacher.[2] And discipleship involves the process of following. This was how the term *disciple* was used in New Testament times and helps us understand how people then might have understood its meaning. The great teacher could have been a philosopher or even a religious thinker who challenged his disciples with his teaching. The relationship between the teacher and his disciples could be distant (simply a teacher-student intellectual kind of relationship) or it could be close—in some cases the disciple lived with the teacher and mimicked his behavior.

Evaluation. If we compare this model with that in the New Testament, we discover some similarities and discrepancies. First, there were those who considered Jesus to be their teacher and themselves learners, but they were not believers in him. When his teaching became difficult for them, they abandoned him. An example is found in John 6:53–67 where Jesus teaches the crowds that unless they eat his flesh and drink his blood, they will have no life in them. While Jesus did not mean for this to be taken literally, many of his disciples did not understand this and abandoned him at this point (v. 66). Second, some of his disciples had a distant relationship with Jesus (such as those in John 6:53–67), while others were close, such as the Twelve (see Mark 3:14). Consequently, due to the discrepancies, this model may prove more confusing than helpful.

Four Views
of Disciple Making

Disciples are learners.

Committed Believers

Based on my ministry and research, the most common view of discipleship within the seminary and the churches, currently and in the past few centuries, is that a disciple is a committed believer. Those who hold this view argue that a disciple is a believer in Christ, but a believer is not necessarily a disciple. Thus a disciple is one who has committed his or her life to growing in the faith and serving Jesus, no matter the personal cost. For example, Dwight Pentecost, Bible teacher and retired Dallas Seminary professor, defines *disciple* and *discipleship*:

> There is a vast difference between being saved and being a disciple. Not all men who are saved are disciples although all who are disciples are saved. In discussing the question of discipleship, we are not dealing with a man's salvation. We are dealing with a man's relationship to Jesus Christ as his teacher, his Master, and his Lord.[3]

Author Walter Henrichsen, who serves with The Navigators, says of the believer who has not committed his life to serving Christ:

> See that man? He is a believer who has refused to pay the price of becoming a disciple. In making that decision, he has relegated himself to a life of mediocrity. Given a chance to be first, he has chosen to be last. To use the words of the Lord Jesus, he is savorless salt. Whatever you do, don't be like him.[4]

Leroy Eims, who teaches that the goal of the Christian's life—especially the new Christian—is someday to become a disciple, writes: "The commission of Christ to you was to make disciples, not just get converts. So your objective now is to help this new Christian progress to the point where he is a fruitful, mature, and dedicated disciple."[5] Thus a disciple is a mature, fruitful, dedicated believer. He also writes that typically it takes approximately two years for a new convert to become a disciple.[6]

This model implies that there are basically two kinds or classes of Christians in the church. The first are ordinary believers, and the second are committed believers who are following Christ as his disciples. And all of us who are believers fall into one category or the other.

Evaluation. This model runs into a number of difficulties. I have addressed some near the end of chapter 1. Here I would like to explore this further.

Four Views of Disciple Making

Disciples are learners.

Disciples are committed believers.

SIMPLY BELIEVERS

As we have seen, the Scriptures are clear that a disciple is not necessarily a believer who has committed his or her life to following the Savior, but simply a believer. Committed believers are committed disciples. Uncommitted believers are uncommitted disciples. In the book of Acts, Luke uses the term *disciple* for believers regardless of their commitment to Christ (Acts 6:1–2, 7; 9:1, 26; 11:26; 14:21–22; 15:10; 18:23; 19:9). Let us examine several of these examples.

In Acts 6:1 Luke notes that the Grecian Jews were complaining against the Hebraic Jews because they were being overlooked in the daily distribution of food. And this took place at a time "when the number of disciples was increasing" in Jerusalem. It is clear that he was not talking only about those believers who had committed all to follow Christ but also those who were new converts to the faith. Yet he calls them disciples. Then in verse 7 he notes, "the word of God spread. The number of disciples in Jerusalem increased rapidly, and a large number of priests became obedient to the faith." His point is not that uncommitted believers were becoming committed believers but that unbelievers were becoming believers.

In Acts 9:1 Luke writes, "Meanwhile, Saul was still breathing out murderous threats against the Lord's disciples." He is not saying that Saul (Paul) was threatening only the committed, mature believers but all believers regardless of their commitment to Christ. And in verse 26 he writes that when the newly converted Saul approached the church in Jerusalem, "he tried to join the disciples, but they were all afraid of him, not believing that he really was a disciple." Again, if we attempt to place those who had made a strong commitment to follow Jesus in this passage, it would not make sense. You would have to argue that he tried to join only the mature believers and that they were afraid of him because they were not convinced that he was a committed Christian.

In Acts 11:26 Luke writes, "The disciples were called Christians first at Antioch." If he were talking only about deeply committed believers, then we would have to assume that those believers who were not as committed were not called Christians.

I could make the same or a similar argument from Acts 14:21–22; 15:10; 18:23; and 19:9. Without question, disciples in the book of Acts were synonymous with believers. Much of Jesus's teaching in the Gospels focuses on the need for his disciples to make the deepest of commitments to him (see Matt. 16:24–26; Luke 13:34–35). But the concept of biblical discipleship begins when a person accepts Christ. Then the new disciple needs to become a committed, growing disciple.

ONLY ONE CLASS OF CHRISTIAN

The Bible does not teach that there are two kinds or classes of Christians that make up Christ's church. Scripture does not draw a line in the sand between ordinary Christians and active Christians. If this were the case, we would have to ask, Where do you draw the line? This question is similar to the one we ask of those who profess a works salvation. If salvation is by works, where do you draw the line? Would God let someone into heaven who has done 1,000 good works but slam the door on one who has done only 999? Would he distinguish between one believer who has committed more of his or her life to Christ and another who has committed slightly less to the Savior? Take, for example, the spiritual disciplines. How many of the spiritual disciplines would one have to practice to be considered a true disciple?

The ultimate goal of the Great Commission is to produce mature believers. Once a person comes to faith, he or she begins the journey toward maturity. The reality is that all Christians are living at some point along the discipleship or maturity continuum (covered at the end of chapter 1). Some are farther along and more committed than others.

Ministers

This model believes that disciples are those Christians who give their lives to go into the ministry, the ones God has called to full-time, professional ministry. They are the pastors and staff who serve as the paid professionals in the typical church. Those who hold this view equate the call to radical discipleship with the call to ministry. They would also equate today's pastors and staff with the Twelve. Thus today's ministers would be trained much as Jesus trained and commissioned the Twelve in Matthew 10.

Evaluation. The Scriptures that I applied to the previous model would apply to this one. They show that the Bible does not identify two classes of Christians. And the belief that disciples are only those called for full-time ministry or service to the Savior is another problem.

Four Views of Disciple Making
Disciples are learners.
Disciples are committed believers.
Disciples are ministers.

Converts Who Make Christ Lord

This model represents the view of those who believe in lordship salvation. Next to the second model presented above, this is the most common view in Christian circles today. When believers place their faith in Christ, they must agree to make Christ Lord of their lives to be saved. Grace is free, but it is not cheap. Thus, according to many who hold this view, the unbeliever must place his faith in Christ and agree to a life of discipleship and service to Christ to be saved.

Evaluation. There are numerous problems with this model. First, salvation is by faith in Christ alone (John 3:16; Eph. 2:8–9). To argue that, in addition, one must agree to serve Christ as his disciple is to add a second requirement for salvation. This does not square with grace.

Second, how can a lost person even understand such a commitment, much less make it? Scripture teaches that a lost person does not accept the things that come from the Spirit, because he regards them as foolishness, and he cannot possibly understand them because they are discerned only by those who have the Spirit (1 Cor. 2:14). A lost person does not have the Spirit dwelling within him (Rom. 8:9). Paul teaches in verses 6–8 that the mind of the lost person is death, is hostile to God, does not submit to God's law, and cannot please God.

Third, it's a question again of degree. What does it mean to agree to a life of discipleship? What does that entail? Does one have to commit to live a reasonably good life, or does one have to agree to leave family and friends to follow Jesus as the disciples did in the Gospels (Matt. 19:27, 29)?

Fourth, what happens when a person has supposedly agreed to make Christ Lord (whatever that means), yet he or she fails to follow through with the commitment? Does that mean the person is not saved or was not saved? The problem with this view is that even Paul struggled with sin as a believer, for he writes in Romans 7:14: "We know that the law is spiritual; but I am unspiritual, sold as a slave to sin."

Finally, Charles Ryrie writes:

> Confusion enters when we attempt to take the conditions for spiritual growth and make them conditions for becoming a disciple, or when we make the characteristics of the life of discipleship conditions for entering the life of a disciple. In Luke 14:16–24 He related the parable of the great supper into which entrance was unrestricted, free and for all. In Luke 14:25–33 He taught the restrictions of the life that continues to follow Him in the continuing process of discipleship, and they were very strict. To make these conditions for the life of service requirements for acquiring the life is to confuse the gospel utterly by muddying the clear waters of the grace of God with the works of man.[7]

Four Views of Disciple Making

Disciples are learners.

Disciples are committed believers.

Disciples are ministers.

Disciples are converts who have agreed to make Christ Lord of their lives.

What Disciple Making Is

The four models presented above help us to clarify and fine-tune our definition of *disciple making* by determining what it is not. Now it is time to focus on the definitions of a *disciple* and *discipleship* to discover what disciple making is.

Disciple

THE GENERAL MEANING

Wilkins is correct when he argues that the definition of a disciple must be understood in both a general and a specific sense.[8] In a general sense a disciple, according to Scripture, is *a committed follower of a person,* such as a teacher or master.[9] Examples are the disciples who followed Moses (John 9:28), the disciples of John the Baptist (Matt. 9:14), and the Twelve. In Mark 1:17 Jesus said to Simon Peter and his brother Andrew, "Come, follow me, and I will make you fishers of men." Later on the same day James and John were fishing with their father, and Jesus approached them. Matthew writes, "Jesus called them, and immediately they left the boat and their father and followed him" (Matt. 4:21–22). In Mark 2:14 Jesus said to Levi (Matthew), "Follow me." And in John 1:43 Jesus said to Philip, "Follow me."

Finally, the persons whom some disciples follow may not be believers in Christ, such as the Pharisees who had their own disciples (Matt. 22:16; Mark 2:18); and some who are called disciples are not believers (John 6:53–66).

THE SPECIFIC MEANING

In a specific sense, a disciple is one who has trusted in Christ as Savior. In short, he or she is a *believer in Christ* or a Christian (other perfectly acceptable biblical terms are "brother," "sister," "saint," and so on). We discovered this above as well as in chapter 1, when we studied the use of the term *disciple* in the book of Acts. This is so important to this discussion that it bears repeating: a disciple may be a deeply committed believer who is "sold out" to Christ; however, a disciple may also *not* be a *committed* believer, but still a believer in Christ. Committed disciples are committed believers, and uncommitted disciples are uncommitted believers. What both have in common is that they share a faith in Christ as Savior.

But one might object to this definition based on such passages as Luke 14:25–26 where Luke writes, "Large crowds were traveling with Jesus, and turning to them he said: 'If anyone comes to me and does not hate his father and mother, his wife and children, his brothers and sisters—yes, even his own life—he cannot be my disciple.'" The key to understanding such passages is knowing not only the context but also to whom Jesus is speaking. Here he is speaking to the large crowds that were made up primarily of unbelievers or nondisciples, and he is talking about how to become a disciple or believer. But how does this square with grace? I will address this further in chapter 5.

Discipleship

The term *discipleship* is not found in Scripture, much to the amazement of many Christians. It is an English word that comes from the terms *disciple* and *disciples*. Thus its meaning is not derived from biblical usage but from how Christians have used it over the years. If we want to use it biblically, we must use it to describe the ongoing life of a disciple (believer in Christ) that involves following the Savior and becoming more like him. People become disciples through evangelism. Then they grow as Christians through the process of discipleship. To talk about Christian discipleship properly, we must use the term to refer to the growth of a disciple (Christian) in every area of his or her life.

Note that I have referred to discipleship as a process. The Christian is always in process, which will include setbacks as well as progress toward Christian maturity. Michael Wilkins writes:

> . . . conversion marks the beginning point of discipleship, not a later point of commitment or a process of spiritual growth. Degrees of maturity will be realized as one traverses the discipleship path, but all true believers are disciples on that path. Therefore, evangelism is the starting point for making disciples. Jesus said that we are to make disciples of all "nations," not to make disciples of those who are already believers. With Luke's additional insights, we can see that prospective converts must somehow be challenged to count the cost of the life of discipleship.[10]

Disciple Making

Based on the two concepts of a disciple and discipleship, we can now describe true disciple making. The process of making disciples involves leading unbelievers to faith in Christ so that they become disciples (Christians). Disciple making must not end with a person's conversion, however. It's an ongoing process that encourages the believer (whether a new believer or an uncommitted Christian) to follow Christ and become more like him. When we become more like Christ, we mature as Christians, which is the goal of making disciples (Eph. 4:13–15; Col. 1:28).

Questions for Reflection and Discussion

1. Of the four models that illustrate four views of discipleship, did you find one or more that reflect your view? If so, how would you respond to the author's critique of your view? If not, why not?
2. Of the four models, which, if any, would be the view held by your congregation? If you are not the pastor, which, if any, would reflect his or her view? If you are the pastor and your view differs with that of the board and/or congregation, what will you do about this?
3. Did the section on the four views sharpen and refine your view of discipleship? If so, how?
4. Do you agree with the author when he says that model 2 is the most common view today on discipleship? Is it or was it your view? If so, have you, by any chance, begun to rethink your view or even change your view? If not, why not?
5. If you know people (friends, pastor, church people) who hold to one or several of the four models, will you engage them in conversation over their views? Why or why not? How might you help them to examine their view in light of Scripture?
6. Do you agree with the author's definitions and explanation of the terms *disciple* and *discipleship*? Why or why not?

4

WHOSE JOB IS IT?

The Responsibility for Making Disciples

So far each chapter has addressed a crucial, preparatory question in the disciple-making process. The question in this chapter is, Where does the responsibility for disciple making rest? In short, who makes disciples? I believe that the responsibility for disciple making falls in three domains. In order of importance, they are God, the individual disciple or Christian, and the local church.

God's Responsibility

First, and the most important of those responsible for making disciples, is God. So we must ask, where is God in the process? What is his role in disciple making?

If God is not involved in the process of disciple making, it will not happen. That's how essential his role is. Some hold the view that disciple making is all up to God. Their philosophy is "let go and let God." Those who subscribe to this view believe that the primary problem to seeing things accomplished for God is that far too often his people get in the way. Thus the solution is for us to "let go" in our futile efforts to serve the Savior and "let God" do his work. These people would encourage us to get out of God's way and watch God do his work of discipleship.

Who Is Responsible
for Making Disciples?

The Godhead (Trinity)

Another view goes to the opposite extreme. It places most of the responsibility on God's people to get God's work done. The idea is that while God wants to accomplish his plans, he wants to do so mostly through believers. People who hold this view may virtually move God out of the picture. This is a form of deism—believing that God created the heavens and earth and then deserted them, leaving them to operate on their own.

While there may be some truth in both positions, the biblical truth lies somewhere in the middle. Scripture affirms that God has not abandoned his people, and in the form of the Godhead, all three members of the Trinity are involved in the disciple-making process.

God the Father

In 1 Corinthians 3:5–7 Paul clarifies the roles that God and his people play in growing his church. He writes, "What, after all, is Apollos? And what is Paul? Only servants, through whom you came to believe—as the Lord has assigned to each his task. I planted the seed, Apollos watered it, but God made it grow. So neither he who plants nor he who waters is anything, but only God, who makes things grow."

We must note that each plays a role in the process. None can be left out. Paul writes that his role was to plant the seed of faith, and Apollos's role was to water it. But God's role was to cause it to grow. Thus all are involved in some way, but God's role is essential to the process.

It is important to observe here that Paul uses a plant metaphor to get his point across. Those of us who are weekend gardeners can identify quickly with this illustration. I am one of those rare individuals who likes to work in his yard. There is something special to planting grass in bare spots, trimming bushes, and coordinating various colored plants with one another. All these things I can and should do if I want to have a healthy, attractive yard, yet I cannot make my grass and bushes grow. I am totally dependent on God "who makes things grow."

Another passage that spells out God's part and man's part is Proverbs 21:31: "The horse is made ready for the day of battle, but victory rests with the LORD." Using a war metaphor that most Israelites would understand, the writer states that our role is to make sure the horse is ready when it is time to go into battle. All good military people understand that you do not go into battle unprepared. However, regardless of our preparation or the lack thereof, we must understand that it is God, and not we, who gives the victory. Thus we have an important role, and he has an even more important key role. The same is true in the disciple-making process. God makes his people grow.

God the Son

In Matthew 16, in response to Jesus's question, Peter said, "You are the Christ, the Son of the living God" (v. 16). Then after Jesus pronounced a blessing on Peter, he used a building metaphor to teach about his church: "I will build my church, and the gates of Hades will not overcome it" (v. 18). When Jesus speaks of building his church, it is not a reference to a literal building or, as some profess, the Roman Catholic Church. It is a reference to making disciples (seeing people come to faith in Christ and then grow in their faith). Jesus is still at work building his church in the twenty-first century, as he was in the first century when he uttered these words. Without him there would be no church.

Some who are aware of the tremendous struggles that the church is facing in the twenty-first century might be tempted by this passage to ask what has happened to this church that Jesus said he is building. Recently, at a pastors' conference, I heard Tony Evans—author, Bible conference speaker, and pastor of Oak Cliff Bible Fellowship in Dallas, Texas—address this problem. His answer is that maybe today's struggling churches are not Christ's church but someone else's church.

God the Holy Spirit

In 2 Corinthians 3:1–6 Paul asserts that should he need some kind of recommendation, his ministry to the church at Corinth was his letter of recommendation. Then he says, "Such confidence as this is ours through Christ before God. Not that we are competent in ourselves to claim anything for ourselves, but our competence comes from God. He has made us competent as ministers of a new covenant" (vv. 4–6). Here Paul is making sure that God gets the credit for Paul's ministry at Corinth. Yet at the same time he acknowledges his part in the process, calling other ministers and himself "competent as ministers of a new covenant."

Next, 2 Corinthians 3:17–18 captures best God's role and work in the discipleship (Christian growth) process. Paul says to the church at Corinth, "Now the Lord is the Spirit, and where the Spirit of the Lord is, there is freedom. And we, who with unveiled faces all reflect the Lord's glory, are being transformed into his likeness with ever-increasing glory, which comes from the Lord, who is the Spirit." Paul makes it crystal clear that God the Holy Spirit is the one who is in the transformation business, not believers. And the Spirit's work of discipleship in the church is to transform the Corinthians back then and us now into Christ's likeness. As we are progressively being transformed by the Holy Spirit into Christ's likeness, we show forth the fruit of the Spirit (Gal.

5:22–23) in our lives. This is the ultimate goal of our discipleship process—to follow and become like Christ.

The Disciple's Responsibility

Each Christian is responsible for his or her own development as a disciple of Christ. While the Godhead is involved in making disciples, we can still resist those efforts and thus circumvent the process. This involves the freedom of man's will. There are several theological positions on the freedom of the human will to make decisions that affect one's life. I suspect that in light of the ravages of sin, most would agree that man does not have a will that is completely and totally free. Sin has affected all of us to some degree. Still, various theologians argue different positions on the extent of the freedom of the human will. Some believe that man has little or no freedom, while others argue for a limited freedom.

**Who Is Responsible
for Making Disciples?**

The Godhead (Trinity)

The Disciple

It is not the purpose of this book or this chapter to solve this thorny theological debate. Regardless of where one stands on the issue, all or most would agree that God holds people responsible for their decisions, whether they are believers or unbelievers. An example would be Israel's refusal to obey and honor God. Jesus says in Matthew 23:37: "O Jerusalem, Jerusalem, you who kill the prophets and stone those sent to you, how often I have longed to gather your children together, as a hen gathers her chicks under her wings, but *you were not willing*" (italics mine). Here we see what God was willing or longing to do for the people and how they resisted his efforts. He was willing, but they were not.

Scripture teaches clearly that the disciple or Christian can resist God due to sin. Jesus died and thus paid for our sins on the cross, but that does not mean that we are free from sin. We are free from the penalty of but not the power of sin in our lives. Through his death on the cross, Jesus broke the reigning power of sin over our lives. Thus the answer to Paul's question for the believer in Romans 6:1, "Shall we go on sinning?" is no. Paul goes on to explain in verse 6 that when Christ died, our old self was crucified with him so that we would no longer have to serve sin. That is the upside of discipleship. And there is a downside. We can choose to continue to serve sin. Thus Paul appeals to us in verses 12–14 to present ourselves to God as instruments of his righteousness. And he says much the same in Romans 12:1, where he urges us to offer our bodies "as living sacrifices, holy and pleasing to God." That is how we serve God and not sin.

The New Testament includes many passages that instruct the disciple on how to live in a way that honors God. And many of them are commands that imply that a disciple can choose to disobey as well as obey. Therefore, Scripture clearly holds each disciple responsible for the pursuit of the discipleship process in his or her life. No disciple will be able to arrive at the end of life and say that he or she wanted to grow to maturity but did not have a choice in the matter.

I am convinced that one of the great problems facing today's churches in growing disciples is that too few disciples are taking personal responsibility for their own spiritual growth and development. Willow Creek Community Church discovered this when they surveyed their congregation.[1] People are depending on the church and its ministries to accomplish this for them. And many churches tend to believe that this is totally their responsibility to their people! The problem is that when it does not happen, who gets the blame? It is the church and not the disciple. Churches need to understand and accept their role in training disciples, as covered in the next section, and then teach their people to take responsibility for their own spiritual growth. You will find in the next section that the church's disciple-making responsibility is to come alongside and complement what each person is doing personally to grow and mature in the faith.

Since it is imperative that each Christian and member of a church have a plan for personal spiritual development, what might such a plan look like? This broaches the topic of the doctrine of sanctification. The problem is that there are many views as to how a believer is sanctified or matures in his or her faith. It depends on one's theology. Consequently, much of the following depends on the leadership of the church and their theology of sanctification. I believe that most leaders would agree that the following elements should be included in a personal plan of discipleship: Bible reading, individual worship, prayer, serving, stewardship or generosity, loving people, evangelism, and spiritual disciplines such as solitude, confession of sin, meditation, and simplicity. At the very end of chapter 6, I discuss some practical ways for a church to implement such a plan for individual discipleship.

The Church's Responsibility

Finally, not only does the Godhead and each disciple have responsibility for making disciples, but the church has a part as well. Here I want to make a distinction between the responsibility of each disciple for his or her own discipleship and the church's responsibility in making disciples. Whereas each individual is responsible for making a choice as to whether he or she will be a growing disciple, the church as a body is responsible for helping its people grow as disciples. The role of the disciple in deciding is personal and individual. The role of the church in deciding for others is public and corporate. It is this last emphasis that I want to develop here. The latter assumes and builds on the former. The church can provide a process of discipleship only for those individuals who are willing to be a part of such a process, whether they are many or few. The church is to come alongside and help. Perhaps Home Depot's slogan articulates it best: "You can do it, and we can help!"

> The Role of the Disciple—personal and individual
> The Role of the Church—public and corporate

Making Disciples

According to Matthew 28:19–20, the church as the body of Christ is to play a major role in making disciples. Jesus addresses this passage to the disciples, as both disciples and apostles. Wilkins comments:

> Although the Twelve were both disciples and apostles, scholars agree that the terms *disciple* and *apostle* point to significantly different aspects. Indeed, while in the Gospels the Twelve are almost always called disciples, in the book of Acts the Twelve are never called disciples. In Acts they are only called apostles, to emphasize their leadership role in the early church.[2]

Thus Jesus directs this passage not only to the disciples as future founding members and examples to the church but to the apostles as the key leaders of the coming church. There is no doubt the Great Commission is for the church and not just the disciples, as some argue.

> **Who Is Responsible**
> **for Making Disciples?**
>
> The Godhead (Trinity)
> The Disciple
> **The Church**

Jesus clearly and expressly commanded the apostles as leaders of the church to set the example and make disciples. They are to make more of what the Savior had made of them. It is a call to spiritual reproduction. To accomplish this commission, each church needs to develop its own unique process of disciple making and communicate this to its people. It is imperative that everyone in the church know and understand the church's process for making disciples (evangelism) and maturing them (sanctification). And this is the reason I developed the Maturity Matrix (see p. 96) to help the church accomplish this task.

The Body of Christ

Nowhere does the Bible encourage "lone ranger" Christians. As the church, we need one another. Discipleship is a group process, involving all the body of Christ. We cannot grow and mature alone.

While I will argue that all believers need the body, I do realize that many in the body are not convinced of this. Barna writes:

> Fewer than one out of every five adults firmly believes that a congregational church is a critical element in their spiritual growth. . . . Only 17% of adults said that "a person's faith is meant to be developed by involvement in a local church." Even evangelicals and born-again Christians generally dismissed that notion: only one-third of all evangelicals . . . endorsed the concept.[3]

I have assumed in the past that those who drop out of church are mostly unbelievers or carnal Christians. Barna states that, while some are carnal Christians, a growing proportion (perhaps the majority) are deeply committed believers who leave their churches because they want more of God but are not getting it in their local church.[4] When Willow Creek Community Church surveyed their congregation, they discovered much the same. The segment of their spiritual continuum that consists of the most mature people in the church reported, "My faith is central to my life and I'm trying to grow, but my church is letting me down."[5]

What a sad commentary on churches in North America! Apparently far too many are proving a detriment to discipleship. It is most likely that such caustic churches do more harm than good to the faith of their congregations. Regardless, though healthy churches have become fewer in number over the past few years, we must not overlook the fact that there are many still out there. This simply becomes another argument for planting growing, healthy, vibrant churches that cultivate their disciples as well as for revitalizing unhealthy churches to the point that they begin to cultivate disciples.

Not only is the church to make disciples, but in 1 Corinthians 12:12–31 Paul makes the strongest of arguments that we need the church—the body of Christ—for this to happen. Individually we are responsible for our own spiritual growth, but the church can and is to help. Embracing the metaphor of the human body to make his point, he says that each believer is a specific body part, such as the foot, the hand, the ear, and the eye. Then in verses 21–23, he writes:

> The eye cannot say to the hand, "I don't need you!" And the head cannot say to the feet, "I don't need you!" On the contrary, those parts of the body that seem to be weaker are indispensable, and the parts that we think are less honorable we treat with special honor. And the parts that are unpresentable are treated with special modesty.

Why does Paul make this argument? Why do we need other believers who make up the local body of Christ? The reason is found in the "one another" passages spread across several New Testament Epistles. There are some fifty such biblical references, many of which encourage believers to love one another (Rom. 12:10; 13:8; 1 Peter 1:22; 1 John 3:11, 23; 4:7, 11). I would also include under the love grouping the passages that encourage the church to greet one another with a holy kiss (Rom. 16:16; 1 Cor. 16:20; 2 Cor. 13:12). The key to understanding what these mean is the exhortation found in 1 Peter 5:14 where Peter writes: "Greet one another with a kiss of love." It is a physical way of showing or expressing love for one another in the body.

Here is a sampling of the "one another" passages:

Honor one another (Rom. 12:10).

Live in harmony with one another (Rom. 12:16).

Let us stop passing judgment on one another (Rom. 14:13).

Accept one another (Rom. 15:7).

Wait for each other (1 Cor. 11:33).

Have equal concern for each other (1 Cor. 12:25).

Serve one another (Gal. 5:13).

Let us not become conceited, provoking and envying one another (Gal. 5:26).

Be patient, bearing with one another in love (Eph. 4:2).

Be kind and compassionate to one another, forgiving each other (Eph. 4:32).

Submit to one another (Eph. 5:21).

Do not lie to each other (Col. 3:9).

Bear with each other (Col. 3:13).

Teach and admonish one another with all wisdom (Col. 3:16).

Encourage one another (1 Thess. 5:11; Heb. 10:25).

Build each other up (1 Thess. 5:11).

Encourage one another daily (Heb. 3:13).

Spur one another on toward love and good deeds (Heb. 10:24).

Do not slander one another (James 4:11).

Don't grumble against each other (James 5:9).

Confess your sins to each other (James 5:16).

Pray for each other (James 5:16).

Live in harmony with one another (1 Peter 3:8).

Offer hospitality to one another (1 Peter 4:9).

Clothe yourselves with humility toward one another (1 Peter 5:5).

Paul and other writers place a strong emphasis on the "love one another" passages (at least eleven references). And the other "one another" passages above are telling us how to love each other in the church. The point is that all believers need the body and need to be loved by that body if discipleship is to occur. Where else in this world will we find such love that is so vital to our spiritual and emotional health as developing, maturing disciples of Christ?

Consequently, the answer to the problem of weak churches that are not implementing or following Christ's command to make disciples is not to abandon the church, as many seem to be doing. This is unbiblical. The answer, instead, is to plant disciple-making churches and do everything within our power as church leaders to revitalize struggling churches.

Questions for Reflection and Discussion

1. The author believes that God, the individual believer, and the church are all responsible for making disciples in obedience to the Great Commission. Do you agree? Why or why not? Can you think of any other entity that might have a role in making disciples? If so, who or what?

2. What is God's role in making disciples? How does his role work with our role? Does he expect us to do it all? Should we expect him to do it all—are we to "let go and let God"? Why or why not?

3. What is our role as disciples and believers in seeing that we become mature disciples? How much responsibility do we have in the process? If we have opportunity and do not follow through, who is to blame?

4. What is the church's role in making disciples? Does your church have a carefully thought-through disciple-making process? Why or why not? If so, does the congregation know and understand what it is? If not, what do you plan to do about this?

5. Do you believe that individual believers really need the church as the loving body of Christ? Why or why not? Do you need the church in your life? Why or why not?

5

How Did Jesus Make Disciples?

Biblical Disciple Making, Part 1

One of the important issues that is vital to discipleship is how our churches should go about making disciples. What is to be our discipleship methodology? In addition, our goal is not only to develop a simple, clear strategy for making authentic disciples, but we want it to be a biblical methodology. To accomplish this we must turn to the Scriptures to discover what the Bible teaches about disciple making.

Jesus said much about making disciples in the Gospels, and the church addresses the issue in Acts and the Epistles. There are two schools of thought. Some argue strongly that we should make disciples the way Jesus did. Jesus's methodology set the standard for all others, and the early church simply followed suit. Others argue that if we study the church's methodology in the book of Acts and the Epistles, we will see that it made disciples differently than Jesus did.

When we study discipleship in the Gospels, the book of Acts, and the Epistles, we will note both similarities and differences. In this chapter I will investigate and show how Jesus made disciples. Then in the next chapter I will show how the early church made disciples and compare their method to Jesus's approach in an attempt to arrive at a biblical viewpoint that will help us with our methodology for disciple making.

It makes perfect sense, if we want to know how to make disciples, to study how Jesus—the master disciple maker—went about this task. To understand his methodology, we must first look at his message of discipleship.

Jesus's Message of Discipleship

I have divided this section on Jesus's message of discipleship into two parts. First, we will discover to whom he spoke; then we'll examine what he said to them.

His Audiences

Hermeneutics addresses how we interpret the Bible. And there are a number of hermeneutical principles that will help us interpret well the Scriptures. For example, one principle that will help us as we examine Jesus's teaching is that we must interpret a passage of Scripture in its context. We must ask, What do the passages that make up the surrounding context say that will help us understand our passage? I suspect that most false teaching is the result of taking passages out of their proper context.

In attempting to discern Jesus's message of discipleship and ultimately how he made disciples, it is critical to identify his audience. The importance of his audience will become even more evident when we examine what he taught. We must ask, When Jesus spoke, who was listening? To whom was he speaking, and why? At various times Jesus's audience was the crowd, the disciples, or a combination of the two.

THE CROWDS

Practically everywhere Jesus went throughout his public ministry, he drew large crowds (Matt. 8:1, 18; 12:46; 13:1–2; Mark 1:33, 45; 2:2, 13; 3:7–9, 20, 32; 4:1, 36; and so on). Much of his early public ministry involved healing and casting out demons, as well as teaching that addressed the issues of his day, and this obviously attracted much attention (Mark 1:28). While the size of these crowds likely varied, we get an idea of how big they could get from the feeding of the five thousand. They consisted mostly of Jewish people who were not disciples (believers). And the purpose of Jesus's ministry was to reach them and see them become disciples (Matt. 9:35–38).

The crowds literally followed Jesus from place to place, but they did so primarily for what he could do for them: heal them, teach them, cast out their demons, and so on. And this was okay, because this is the reason he had come to them (Mark 1:38). Some of these people became disciples (Matt. 8:18–22; 17:14–15—the father was probably a disciple, because he called Jesus "Lord"); others became his opponents and went so far as to laugh at him (9:23–24) and accept the responsibility for his death (27:24–25).

THE DISCIPLES

A second audience was Jesus's disciples (Matt. 5:1–2; 11:1; Mark 8:31; 10:32; John 13–17). Unlike the crowds, the disciples were those who obeyed Jesus's call to follow him and became believers in him. They consisted of two groups: the narrow circle and a broader circle.

The narrow circle were the Twelve who made up the core of his disciples. They ranged in occupation from fisherman to tax collector, and these are the men he called to follow him (see, for example, Mark 1:16–20), who later came to faith in him (John 2:11). To follow him, they had to leave their families, friends, property, and occupations (Matt. 19:27, 29). They entered into a special relationship with him and became the main focus of his ministry after he turned his attention from the crowds (John 13–17). This was a time of preparation for their role as apostles and future leaders who would lead the church, as seen in the book of Acts.

A study of the Twelve shows that they were divided into smaller groups with a leader of each. And one of these groups consisted of the brothers Peter and Andrew and James and John. They formed an inner circle that traveled with Jesus on special occasions. Peter was not only the leader of the inner circle but of the Twelve (Matt. 10:2).

The broader circle of disciples consisted of a variety of men and women, some in groups and others as individuals, who followed Jesus and believed in him. Luke makes reference to a group of men from whom Jesus chose the Twelve (Luke 6:13) and a group of women who helped support Jesus and the Twelve (8:1–3). Then there are a number of individual disciples, such as Zacchaeus, the tax collector (19:1–10); a demon-possessed man (Mark 5:18–19); Joseph of Arimathea (Matt. 27:57; John 19:38); and Nicodemus (John 3:1–21).

Jesus's Circle of Disciples

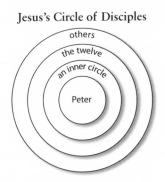

BOTH THE DISCIPLES AND THE CROWDS

There are several instances when Jesus spoke to both his disciples and the crowds together in the same audience. For example, Mark 8:31 tells us that Jesus began to teach the Twelve. Then Mark notes later in verse 34 that

Jesus included the crowd: "Then he called the crowd to him along with his disciples." In Luke we read that Jesus spoke to a large group of his disciples and the crowd (6:17–19). Then at the end of this teaching session, Luke tells us that Jesus did this "in the hearing of the people" (7:1).

Jesus's Primary Audiences

The Crowds

The Disciples

The Disciples and the Crowds

His Messages to His Audiences

Now that we have identified Jesus's audiences, it is important that we examine the key passages that address what he said to each of these three audiences. Since this is a study of discipleship, we will examine Jesus's key teachings but not all passages that relate in some way to discipleship. These key messages are found in the following references: Matthew 4:19; 8:18–22; 10:24–25; 16:24–26; 20:25–28; Mark 1:17; 8:34–38; Luke 5:27–28; 6:40; 9:23–25, 57–62; 14:25–33; John 1:43; 8:31–32; 12:26; 13:34–35; 15:8.

WHAT JESUS TAUGHT THE CROWD

Jesus focused one message specifically on the crowd that consisted mostly of unbelievers. It is found in Luke 14:25–33, where Luke writes:

> Large crowds were traveling with Jesus, and turning to them he said: "If anyone comes to me and does not hate his father and mother, his wife and children, his brothers and sisters—yes, even his own life—he cannot be my disciple. And anyone who does not carry his cross and follow me cannot be my disciple.
> "Suppose one of you wants to build a tower. Will he not first sit down and estimate the cost to see if he has enough money to complete it? For if he lays the foundation and is not able to finish it, everyone who sees it will ridicule him, saying, 'This fellow began to build and was not able to finish.'
> "Or suppose a king is about to go to war against another king. Will he not first sit down and consider whether he is able with ten thousand men to oppose the one coming against him with twenty thousand? If he is not able, he will send a delegation while the other is still a long way off and will ask for terms of peace. In the same way, any of you who does not give up everything he has cannot be my disciple."

Jesus's point is that before becoming his disciple, one must count the cost of what it will mean to follow him. He tells two parables that illustrate this truth: one about the builder of a tower and one about a king who goes to war. What is the cost? The answer is in verse 33—you have to be willing to give up everything to be Jesus's disciple. Only when a person forsakes all is he totally following Jesus.

An initial look at this passage would seem to support the idea held by many that a person can be a Christian without being a disciple, because Jesus seems to be teaching what one must do to become a disciple: hate one's family, take up one's cross, and follow him.

However, the fact that he is addressing this message to a crowd of unbelievers and discussing how to become a disciple (believer) contradicts this. We have already seen that a disciple is a believer. Therefore, Jesus is teaching the crowd what they must do to become believers. But how might we square hating one's parents and taking up a cross and following Jesus with grace? Is he teaching a works salvation?

Michael Wilkins answers this important question by pointing out that, while Jesus speaks to the crowd, his message must be personalized by each individual according to his or her own life circumstance (whether a believer, or as here, an unbeliever).[1] There are several examples where Jesus demonstrates this personalized approach. One is the account of the rich young man in Matthew 19:16–22. In this incident, the rich young man approached Jesus and asked what he had to do to get eternal life. Jesus answered by saying that he must keep the commandments, and the man responded that he has kept them. Then Jesus instructed him to go and sell his possessions and give the money to the poor. The man's response was to walk away disappointed because he had much wealth and was not willing to give it away.

Again, we might ask the same question as we asked about Luke 14:25–33 above: How does this square with grace? The answer is that Jesus personalizes his message to this man's individual situation. Jesus is telling him that before he is ready to believe in Jesus for salvation, he must address his fixation on his wealth. Wealth is a priority in his life and is preventing him from accepting Jesus as Messiah.

Jesus uses the same personal approach in the parable of the good Samaritan in Luke 10:25–37. An expert in the law challenged Jesus with the question, What must I do to inherit eternal life? As he did with the rich ruler, Jesus refers to the Law, asking the man what is written in it. The man quotes the passage about loving God and loving one's neighbor as oneself; then he asks, "Who is my neighbor?" Jesus responds with the story of the Samaritan who, though he was not a Jew and was even despised by most Jews, went out of his way to help a stranded, injured Jewish man. Jesus uses the story to point out to this Jewish expert in the law that his national feelings of racial superiority were a major obstacle to his truly coming to faith.

So how might this personalization process help us to understand Luke 14:25–33? I believe that Jesus has a goal here that is similar to his goal in the other two passages—the issue is becoming a disciple or coming to faith in Jesus. Jesus personalizes his message to the crowd in Luke 14 so that they might consider certain obstacles that would prevent many from trusting in him. In the situation of some, it is their attachment to family. Jesus knew there were all kinds of good things that could get in the way of one's coming to faith, and family was one of them—especially a Jewish family. At that time a Jewish person who accepted Christ risked alienating his family. Thus Jesus is teaching them that they need first to deal with these familial matters and any other issues of life ("even his own life"), because these things could prevent them from embracing him as Savior.

This need to personalize our conversations with lost people is most apparent today as we seek to win people to the Savior. My experience is that it is rare that a person comes to faith in Christ the very first time I present the gospel. They all have issues that short-circuit their ability to place their trust in Christ. For the Muslim, Jew, or even Catholic, it is often family issues that get in the way. They respond, "My family does not embrace this belief, and if I were to accept Christ, they would disown me." Others are trusting their own good deeds to get them to heaven, and some are very proud of such deeds as giving money to charity or volunteering to feed the hungry. To them the message of salvation by grace through faith in Christ is not what they want to hear. Their faith in their good works is preventing them from accepting by faith Jesus's good work on the cross.

WHAT JESUS TAUGHT THE DISCIPLES

Jesus addressed a number of discipleship-related messages to his disciples. They fall into two categories. The first were those teachings that applied only to their time with Jesus during his earthly ministry. The second related to their ministry, both with Jesus in the Gospels and beyond.

The first category consists primarily of Jesus's teaching in Matthew 10:5–15. They are a series of succinct commands that I have summarized in the following:

1. They were to go only to lost Israel, not to the Gentiles or Samaritans (vv. 5–6).
2. Their message to Israel was "The kingdom of heaven is near" (v. 7).
3. Their ministry involved healing the sick, raising the dead, cleansing lepers, and casting out demons (v. 8).
4. They were to depend on those to whom they ministered for their livelihood. Thus they were not to take with them such items as money, clothes, sandals, or a staff (vv. 9–10).
5. On their journey, they were to stay only with worthy people. They were to give the home their greeting and let their peace rest on it (vv. 11–15).
6. It was also understood, according to Peter's words in Matthew 19:27 and 29, that they would leave behind their families and their professions.

Again, it is most important to note that this teaching applied only to the disciples' missionary outreach to Israel in the Gospels (while Jesus was still on earth), not to the church. Thus anyone who attempts to apply these to his or her ministry today is ripping this material out of its context.

The second category consists of five of Jesus's primary teachings on discipleship that relate to today as well as to his ministry in the Gospels. They address the following: the disciple's call to follow Jesus (Matt. 4:19; Mark 1:17; Luke 5:27–28; John 1:43; 12:26); what it means to follow Jesus (Matt. 20:25–28; John 12:26); how disciples follow him (Matt. 8:18–22; 16:24–26; Luke 9:23–25, 57–62); how one can know that he or she is a true follower (John 8:31–32; 13:34–35; 15:8); and the results of following Jesus (Matt. 4:19).

1. *What are disciples supposed to do?* In Luke 14:25–33, we learn how to become a disciple or a believer in Christ. The next obvious question is, Now that I have become a disciple, what am I supposed to do? We can see the answer in several places in the Gospels where Jesus calls the disciples. In Matthew 4:19 and Mark 1:17 Jesus challenges two of his disciples—the brothers Peter and Andrew—to come and follow him. He does the same with Levi (Matthew) in Luke 5:27 and Philip in John 1:43. The capstone to these passages is found in John 12:26 where Jesus says, "Whoever serves me must follow me; and where I am, my servant also will be. My Father will honor the one who serves me." Once a person becomes a disciple, he or she is to follow Jesus. Jesus's invitation is clear: come and follow me!

2. *What does it mean to follow Jesus?* What does following him entail? What is the essence of discipleship? If we were to put discipleship into a beaker and boil it down to its essence, what would we find? I think we would find servanthood, the very essence of discipleship. Disciples are servants. In John 12:26 Jesus associates "followership" with servanthood and stresses the importance of servanthood. Discipleship is all about service. And in Matthew 20:26–28 Jesus uses his own example of what servanthood looks like: "whoever wants to become great among you must be your servant, and whoever wants to be first must be your slave—just as the Son of Man did not come to be served, but to serve, and to give his life as a ransom for many." Disciples of Christ are first his servants, who are willing to serve even to the point of death—the ultimate form of service.

   Though not specifically mentioned in the text, I believe that obedience to Christ is understood. What do servants do? They obey their masters. What do we as servants do? We obey Christ, our Master. And this ties in well to Jesus's mandate in Matthew 28:20: "obey everything I have commanded you."

3. *How do disciples follow Jesus?* In Matthew 16:24–26 (which is the same event as found in Luke 9:23–25), Jesus answers the question. He says to his disciples:

> If anyone would come after me, he must deny himself and take up his cross and follow me. For whoever wants to save his life will lose it, but whoever loses his life for me will find it. What good will it be for a man if he gains the whole world, yet forfeits his soul? Or what can a man give in exchange for his soul?

In this passage Jesus is responding to Peter's rebuke in verse 22. After Jesus explains to the disciples that he must die and be resurrected, Peter takes Jesus aside and rebukes him, saying, "This shall never happen to you!" Jesus responds, "Get behind me, Satan! You are a stumbling block to me; you do not have in mind the things of God, but the things of men." Naturally this leads into our passage where Jesus says that, unlike Peter, the disciples need to deny themselves, take up their crosses, and follow him. Peter is not denying himself and taking up his cross. It is possible that he had become so dependent on Jesus that any thought of not having him physically present was frightening. However, Jesus had taught them earlier, recorded in Mark 9:40, that someone is either for him or against him—there is no middle ground.

We as well as Jesus's first-century disciples must learn to deny ourselves, that is, our will for our lives, and embrace his will for us whatever that may be. This involves our taking up a cross or dying to self. Often those sentenced to die by crucifixion were made to carry part of their cross to the site of crucifixion. I think that this practice is what Jesus is using to illustrate his words.

Jesus provides his disciples with more teaching on how they are to follow him in Matthew 8:18–22 (also in Luke 9:57–62). Jesus teaches certain would-be disciples the importance of putting Jesus ahead of their own personal desires for a place to live and family obligations. In the first instance, a teacher of the law approaches Jesus in verse 19 and states that he will follow him wherever he goes. From Jesus's response in verse 20, we learn that this man does not understand that this would mean being homeless. Jesus's point to the man is that following him would mean living on the fly, much like a homeless person. What Jesus is saying to the man is that he needs to understand the cost and then be willing to pay it, even if it means not having a home.

In the second situation, another person says to Jesus in verse 21 that he must delay his pursuit of discipleship to take care of an important family matter—the burial of his father. In the Near East of the first century, proper burial of a family member, especially the father, was a major concern. Either the father had recently died or the man wanted to delay discipleship until his father eventually died. Regardless, Jesus commands the son to follow him and let someone else bury his father. Again, as in Luke 14:26, family is seen as a potential deterrent to discipleship. Thus Jesus is teaching that we must not allow anything, especially family matters, to block our pursuit of discipleship.

4. *How can one know if he or she is a true disciple of Christ?* What are the marks or characteristics of a true Christ-follower? John's Gospel contains three passages that refer to how followers can truly know that they are Jesus's disciples or believers. John's emphasis both in his Gospel and in his first Epistle is on how one can know if he or she is a Christian. There are evidences for or marks of true discipleship.

The first mark or piece of evidence is found in John 8:31–32, where Jesus states that a true disciple will both believe and hold to his teachings. This means that they agree with his teachings and will not abandon them at some time in the future.

The second mark or piece of evidence is in John 13:34–35. Jesus says that true disciples love one another. Thus one who desires to be a disciple must stop and ask, do I really love other disciples? What is the evidence?

The third mark is found in John 15:8, where Jesus teaches that a true disciple bears fruit. This is similar to Jesus's warning to his disciples in Matthew 7:15–23, where he helps them discern true and false prophets. He says that you can know them by their fruit. False prophets produce thornbushes and thistles (bad works), while good prophets produce grapes and figs (good works).

5. *What is the result of following Jesus?* Now that we know what it will take to follow Jesus, what will be the result of becoming his disciple? The Savior addresses this in both Matthew 4:19 and Mark 1:17. In both of these passages Jesus invites two brothers (Peter and Andrew) to follow him. Then he announces what will be the result of following him: "I will make you fishers of men." I believe this is a reference to disciple making or evangelism, and we see them fishing for men throughout the Gospels. These were fishermen, so they would understand the figure Jesus uses. His point is that you will do little commercial fishing from here on. Instead, you will be fishing for men, which means seeing others become disciples or believers.

What Jesus Taught the Disciples and the Crowd

We learned above that Jesus spoke to his disciples and the crowd about discipleship on two particular occasions. First, in Mark 8:31–33 Jesus teaches the disciples about his coming death. Then he includes the crowd and teaches that, to be his disciples, they must deny themselves, take up their cross, and follow him (vv. 34–38). We learned above that for his disciples this means abandoning our own will for our life and embracing his will for us, whatever that may be. This involves our taking up our cross, or dying to ourselves. But how do you explain Jesus's teaching this to the crowd who are mostly unsaved? We have seen how the message applies to the disciples, but how does it apply to the crowd? Again, Jesus addresses that which is preventing them from believing in him. Here it is their pursuit of their will for themselves instead of his will for them. As long as they hold their agenda over his, they will not come to faith in him. The hope is that some day they will see the futility of pursuing their personal agendas, whatever they may be, and embrace his agenda, which is accepting Jesus as Messiah.

Luke 6:17–7:1 tells of another time when Jesus spoke to both the crowd and the disciples about discipleship issues. As you may recall, in Luke 6:17 Jesus is teaching both a large crowd of his disciples and a great number of people. The content of his message is Luke's equivalent of the beatitudes or blessings found in Matthew 5:3–12, along with other topics, such as loving one's enemies, judging others, discerning good and bad people, and the wise versus the foolish builders. We discover in Luke 7:1 that Jesus taught this in "the hearing of the people." This was a message for his disciples regarding how they should handle various issues. That the crowd heard it does not seem to have made any difference. They heard the message, but there is no indication that it applied to them or that they even understood it.

So what have we learned so far in this chapter about Jesus's major discipleship teaching in the Gospels? Scholar Michael Wilkins says it best: "Overall, discipleship teaching that is directed to the crowds deals with the act of becoming a disciple (evangelism), whereas teaching directed to the disciples deals with growth in discipleship (Christian growth)."[2]

Jesus's Primary Discipleship Messages

To the Crowds
How to become a disciple (believer)—Luke 14:25–33

To the Disciples
Jesus's early ministry only—Matt. 10:5–15
Jesus's early and later ministry
1. What disciples do: they follow Jesus—Matt. 4:19; Mark 1:17; Luke 5:27; John 1:43; 12:26
2. What it means to follow Christ: to serve him—John 12:26; Matt. 20:26–28
3. How disciples follow Jesus: they deny themselves, take up their cross, and follow him—Matt. 16:24–26; Luke 9:23–25; Matt. 8:18–22; Luke 9:57–62
4. The marks of a true disciple: they follow Christ's teaching, love one another, and bear fruit—John 8:31–32; 13:34–35; 15:8
5. The result of following Christ: they become fishers of men or disciple makers—Matt. 4:19; Mark 1:7

To the Crowds and Disciples
Mark 8:31–38; Luke 6:17–7:1

Jesus's Methods of Discipleship

Now that we know Jesus's audiences and his message for them, we need to examine the methods he used to make disciples in the context of those audiences.

Who Made Disciples?

If we use the term *disciple* in a general sense, we will discover that in the Gospels one group and two individuals were the primary disciple makers. The Pharisees as a group made disciples. They are mentioned in Matthew 22:15–16; Mark 2:18; and Luke 5:33. John the Baptist was an individual who had disciples (see Matt. 9:14; Mark 2:18; Luke 5:33; John 1:35; 3:25).

The focus of this section is on the Savior as disciple maker. In the Scriptures there are numerous references to him as the master disciple maker and to his disciples. What I want to point out in the Gospels is that he, and no one else, was the primary maker of disciples. Discipleship in the Gospels took place with Jesus in a personal relationship.

When Did Jesus Make Disciples?

Asking when Jesus made disciples does not refer to the year, month, or days of his activities in the Gospels, as important as they may be. The important thing about the timing is that his disciple making took place before Pentecost. This was a time when the Holy Spirit did not indwell believers on a permanent basis. In John 14:16 Jesus says of the Spirit: "And I will ask the Father, and he will give you another Counselor to be with you forever." This is important because the disciples' understanding of Jesus's teaching was limited prior to Pentecost (see v. 26). However, after Pentecost they would understand much if not all of his teaching (see 16:13). And this would make a significant difference in their ability to make disciples. I will explore this further in the next chapter.

How Did Jesus Make Disciples?

Many believe that the key to our making disciples in the twenty-first century is to follow Jesus's method in the first century. There are at least four ways he went about it, depending on whether he was interacting with a large group (the crowd), a small group (the Twelve), a smaller group (his inner circle), or one-on-one.

He Preached

Jesus preached to the crowd. We must keep in mind that making disciples included evangelism in a large-group context, because one must first *become* a disciple or believer. This was Jesus's goal with the crowds (Matt. 9:35–38). As we discovered earlier in the chapter, Jesus's preaching attracted large crowds, and the primary purpose of his ministry with the crowds was to make them disciples (believers). Jesus's practice was to issue an open call to the crowds (Luke 14:25–27). As we saw earlier, Jesus's message was personalized to the crowd (vv. 25–35), and he used it to call the crowd to make a personal decision to become his disciples. As he preached, the evidence that one had become a disciple was that he or she came out of the crowd and called Jesus "Lord" (Matt. 8:18–21; Luke 17:14–15). Here we note that Jesus addressed discipleship in the context of a large group of people.

He Focused on a Small Group

Jesus poured his life into a small group of disciples, the Twelve whom he had called (see, for example, Mark 1:16–20). In time they came to faith (John 2:11). Initially Jesus ministered publicly to the crowd but individually to the Twelve. Regarding the latter, Mark writes, "He appointed twelve—designating them apostles—that they might be with him and that he might send them out to preach" (Mark 3:14). However, he reached a point where he shifted his ministry away from the crowd and focused primarily on the Twelve (see Mark 9–16) to prepare them as apostles for their leadership ministry in the church after Pentecost. So, with this small group, he pursued discipleship.

He Spent Time Alone with the Inner Circle

Jesus poured his life into an even smaller group, an inner circle of the Twelve. Right after Jesus questioned his disciples about his identity and confronted Peter over his response to Jesus's prediction of his death, he led an inner circle of disciples—Peter, James, and John—up on a mountain, where he was alone with them (Mark 9:2) and where they witnessed his transfiguration (vv. 3–13). Thus Jesus not only discipled the Twelve as a small group but took the inner circle aside for further discipling.

He Counseled Individuals

Jesus counseled a new disciple. I am trying to be careful with the wording here. Note that I am not saying that Jesus discipled an individual. Jesus did not have an ongoing discipling relationship with individuals, but he did counsel, or do a one-time discipling, with individuals, such as Nicodemus (John 3) and Peter (John 21).

In Mark 5:1–20 Jesus cast a demon out of a man who then came to faith. The man insisted on following Jesus, but instead, Jesus instructed him to go home to his family and tell them about his healing and conversion. Jesus could have poured his life into the man as a new disciple (believer) who needed to grow as a disciple, but he did not. This is important because, unlike the encouragement and practice of many today, it does not appear that Jesus discipled many individuals, if any. I do not believe that it is wrong to disciple individuals. At a critical time in my daughter's spiritual development, a young lady discipled her, and to this day my daughter is a strong believer. However, it would seem that a better strategy, in terms of reaching more people, is to minister to large groups of nondisciples (the crowd) and disciple medium and small groups, such as Jesus did with the Twelve and the inner circle. And, of course, in Matthew 28:19 Jesus's challenge is for us to disciple not only unbelievers (evangelism) but the entire church (edification), not just a few individuals who are interested in going further with Christ.

Jesus's Methods for Making Disciples

Jesus preached to the crowds (large group)

Jesus poured his life into the disciples (small group)

Questions for Reflection and Discussion

1. Why does the author think it is important for disciple makers to identify Jesus's audiences when studying his discipleship messages in the Gospels? Do you agree? Why or why not?

2. In Luke 14:25–33 Jesus extends an invitation to the crowd to become his disciples. Since the crowd consists primarily of unbelievers, how does the author explain Jesus's invitation? Do you agree or disagree with the author? Why? Is Jesus teaching that works are somehow involved in salvation? Why or why not? How would you square Jesus's sermon with grace?

3. Do you agree with the author's distinction between Jesus's teaching of the disciples that relates only to his ministry while on earth versus that which applied back then and up to today? Why or why not? What difference does such a distinction make?

4. The author argues that Jesus's teaching that is directed to the crowds deals with the act of becoming a disciple (evangelism), whereas teaching directed to the disciples deals with growth in discipleship (sanctification). Do you agree? Why or why not? How important is it to make this distinction?

5. Why is it important to address the timing of Jesus's making disciples? What difference do Pentecost and the indwelling of the Spirit have on making disciples?

6. What were Jesus's methods for making disciples? Did the author miss any? Can you think of some situations when Jesus discipled individuals?

6

How Did the Church Make Disciples?

Biblical Disciple Making, Part 2

I began the last chapter with this question: What is to be our discipleship methodology? I argued that our methodology should be biblical. In determining a biblical methodology, some argue that we should follow Jesus's disciple-making methodology, while others believe the early New Testament church did it differently and we should follow the church's lead.

In the last chapter I presented a brief study of discipleship in the Gospels, focusing on Jesus's message and methods for making mature disciples. In this chapter I will again do a brief study of discipleship, but in the book of Acts and the Epistles. The purpose is not only to discover how the early church made disciples but to address the similarities and differences between their methods and those in the Gospels. The goal is to arrive at a methodology as well as a biblical viewpoint that addresses how our churches can best make disciples in the twenty-first century.

The Church's Message of Discipleship

The best approach to discover and comprehend the church's message of discipleship is to ask questions in two key areas. First, who was the church's audience for its message? Whom was it trying to reach? Who was listening? Second, what did the church say? What was its message for that audience?

The Church's Audience

We learned that in the Gospels Jesus's message was for Israel. He went first to the house of Israel. The nation was his first target and the audience for his message of discipleship. And when he sent out his disciples, their target was the same audience. In Matthew 10:5–6 he instructed the Twelve, "Do not go among the Gentiles or enter any town of the Samaritans. Go rather to the lost sheep of Israel."

THE JEWS PLUS THE NATIONS

When Jesus commissioned the church, however, he made a change. He added the nations that would include the Gentiles and Samaritans. In Matthew 28:19–20 he instructed the disciples a second time regarding their audience and commanded them, "Go and make disciples of all nations." In Mark 16:15 he said to them, "Go into all the world and preach the good news to all creation." And he further qualified this in Acts 1:8, where he told the disciples to be his witnesses of Christ's resurrection in Jerusalem and in all Judea and Samaria and to the ends of the earth. And this is what the church did. Its audience changed from primarily the Jews in Acts 2–7, to the Samaritans in Acts 8:1, 5, and to Gentiles in Acts 10 and beyond.

THE CROWDS

As the disciples went to the Jews and the nations, they spoke, as Jesus had, to two audiences—the crowds and other disciples. We find a record of Peter's first sermon after Pentecost, beginning in Acts 2:14: "Then Peter stood up with the Eleven, raised his voice and addressed the crowd: 'Fellow Jews and all of you who live in Jerusalem.'" God blessed his sermon, and three thousand people came to faith and were added to the church at Jerusalem (2:41). Again he preached to the crowd in Acts 3:11–26, and five thousand men came to faith in Christ (4:4).

THE DISCIPLES

The disciples and others also spoke to other disciples and to the church. For example, in Acts 1:15 Peter spoke to about 120 disciples, urging them to select an apostle to replace Judas. Then in Acts 4:23–31 Peter and John reported to the church their encounter with the chief priests and Jewish elders and then led the church in a prayer that they would speak God's word with boldness.

Paul's epistles and those of others in the New Testament were addressed to the disciples located in various local churches and were also used for discipleship.

The Church's Message

What was the church's message, and what did it teach about making disciples? The answer is found throughout the Acts and the Epistles. The following passages are just a few examples of what these books teach on discipleship. I will compare them to Jesus's teaching on discipleship in the Gospels to demonstrate that there is much continuity between his teaching and that of the church. I believe that it is likely the church used Jesus's teaching as a foundation for their own teaching on discipleship. Perhaps this was in response to that portion of the Great Commission in Matthew 28:20 where Jesus says, ". . . teaching them to obey everything I have commanded you."

What the Church Taught the Crowd

Jesus taught the crowd how to become disciples (believers). We learned from Jesus's teaching in Luke 14:25–33, where he speaks to the crowd, that each person had to personalize the message according to his or her own life circumstances if the person was to have faith in Jesus and become his disciple. We saw two other examples of this personalization. One is the rich young man in Matthew 19:16–22, and the other is the parable of the good Samaritan in Luke 10:25–37. In any case, the way to become Jesus's disciple is by faith alone. Those who believed in him became his disciples.

We see that the same is true for the church. The church's missionaries taught its crowd how to become believers (disciples). Luke writes in Acts 14:21: "They preached the good news in that city and won a large number of disciples." And again he writes in Acts 6:7: "So the word of God spread. The number of disciples in Jerusalem increased rapidly, and a large number of priests became obedient to the faith."

What the Church Taught the Disciples

The church taught its disciples five general truths about discipleship.

1. *What disciples are supposed to do.* What does God expect? The answer found both in the Gospels and the Epistles is to follow Christ. In Matthew 4:19 and Mark 1:17 Jesus says to Peter and Andrew, "Come, follow me." In Luke 5:27 he says to Levi (Matthew), "Follow me." And in John 1:43 he says the same to Philip, "Follow me." Jesus's many invitations to the disciples were commands to follow him.

   We find a similar concept for the church in 1 Peter 2:21. Peter says to the church, "To this you were called, because Christ suffered for you, leaving you an example, that you should follow in his steps." I believe that Peter is talking about following Jesus's lifestyle in general and suffering in particular. In 1 Corinthians 11:1 Paul underlines the importance of following Christ as well. He exhorts the Corinthian disciples to follow his example as he follows the example of Christ.

2. *What it means to follow Christ.* What is the essence of such following? The answer is service or servanthood. The Savior connects following him with serving him in John 12:26: "Whoever serves me must follow me; and where I am, my servant also will be. My Father will honor the one who serves me." Also note that John 12:26 addresses our serving him, whereas in Matthew 20:26 he adds that we are to serve one another as well: "Not so with you. Instead, whoever wants to become great among you must be your servant." Thus the objects of our service are both the Savior and our fellow disciples.

And this has not changed in the life of the church. First, the church is to serve the Lord. Paul tells the Thessalonian disciples how news had reached him that they had "turned to God from idols to serve the living and true God" (1 Thess. 1:9). Similar passages are Acts 20:19; Romans 12:11; and Colossians 3:24.

Second, the church is to serve others. In Ephesians 4:12 Paul explains to the Ephesian disciples how God has gifted the church so they can "prepare God's people for works of service." Other similar passages are 1 Corinthians 12:5; Ephesians 6:7; and 1 Peter 4:10.

3. *How disciples follow Christ.* Jesus teaches the disciples in Matthew 16:24–25: "If anyone would come after me, he must deny himself and take up his cross and follow me. For whoever wants to save his life will lose it, but whoever loses his life for me will find it." Luke records the same message in Luke 9:23–24. We learned in the last chapter that this means we must put his will and plan for our lives in place of our own, ahead of any personal comfort or family obligations (Matt. 8:18–22). Our life is to become his life. And the life we live must be his life. All of this involves dying to ourselves and our wishes for life and embracing the Savior's will for us.

Paul says much the same to the church in Galatians 2:20: "I have been crucified with Christ and I no longer live, but Christ lives in me. The life I live in the body, I live by faith in the Son of God, who loved me and gave himself for me." Here Paul is addressing his position in Christ and his desire to live his life in accordance with that position. And in Romans 12:1 he says, "Therefore, I urge you, brothers, in view of God's mercy, to offer your bodies as living sacrifices, holy and pleasing to God—this is your spiritual act of worship." He explores this concept more in depth in Romans 6:1–14, teaching the Roman disciples that at the cross Christ broke the power of sin over their lives. Thus, they no longer have to obey sin. Then he challenges them not to offer their bodies to sin but to God. Finally, Paul exhorts in Philippians 3:7–8: "But whatever was to my profit I now consider loss for the sake of Christ. What is more,

I consider everything a loss compared to the surpassing greatness of knowing Christ Jesus my Lord, for whose sake I have lost all things. I consider them rubbish that I may gain Christ."

4. *How people can know they are true disciples.* How can we have assurance of our salvation? In John's Gospel Jesus teaches that true disciples have three characteristics. First, they abide in his word (John 8:31–32). He says to new Jewish disciples, "If you hold to my teaching, you are really my disciples." The term *hold* means both to agree with and not to abandon. A characteristic of disciples in the Jerusalem church, according to Luke, was that "they devoted themselves to the apostles' teaching" (Acts 2:42). Later in Acts 6:1–7 the church faced a problem. The Grecian Jews were being neglected by the Hebraic Jews in the daily distribution of food. The apostles suggested that the church choose seven men to take care of this responsibility. This would free up the apostles' time so they could give attention "to prayer and the ministry of the word" (v. 4). Luke tells his readers in verse 7 that because of this "the word of God spread."

Second, Jesus teaches that true disciples love other disciples: "A new command I give you: Love one another. As I have loved you, so you must love one another. By this all men will know that you are my disciples, if you love one another" (John 13:34–35). John wrote his epistle (1 John) for the purpose of helping believers in the church have assurance of their salvation. To accomplish this he provides them with various tests of faith, one of which is love for one another. In 1 John 3:14 he writes, "We know that we have passed from death to life, because we love our brothers." Thus, love for one's brother is a strong indication that a person is a believer.

The third characteristic of a disciple is fruit bearing. Jesus states, "This is to my Father's glory, that you bear much fruit, showing yourselves to be my disciples" (John 15:8). Fruit bearing both glorifies God and manifests one's discipleship. In Colossians 1:10 Paul writes to the disciples at Colosse: "And we pray this in order that you may live a life worthy of the Lord and may please him in every way: bearing fruit in every good work, growing in the knowledge of God." And in Galatians 5:16–23 Paul teaches that we can know that the Spirit is in control of our lives by the fruit of the Spirit that we produce. He then identifies the fruit as "love, joy, peace, patience, kindness, goodness, faithfulness, gentleness and self-control" (vv. 22–23).

5. *The result of following Christ.* Jesus says that when we follow him, we will become fishers of men. In Matthew 4:19 and Mark 1:17 he says to Peter and Andrew, "Come, follow me, and I will make you fishers of men." In Luke 5 Jesus advises the disciples who are fishing to drop their nets in deeper water. After first objecting, they do so and catch a boatload of fish. Their response is to fear Jesus, and so he says to Peter,

"Don't be afraid; from now on you will catch men" (v. 10). Thus, the catch of fish becomes symbolic of Peter's future ministry to men, when he will make disciples through evangelism. Following Christ produces the result of bringing people to faith.

In Colossians 4:3–4 Paul writes to the church: "And pray for us, too, that God may open a door for our message, so that we may proclaim the mystery of Christ, for which I am in chains. Pray that I may proclaim it clearly, as I should." Paul, who was a mature disciple, had committed his life to making disciples (believers). When we follow Christ, he uses us to reach others. And if we are not reaching others, it is possible we are not following him.

In summary, now that we have studied both Jesus's teaching on discipleship along with the church's teaching, we must revisit the question of whether the church's teaching in Acts and the Epistles was the same as or different from that of the Savior in the Gospels. Did the early church basically carry out what Jesus had begun? Or did the early church take a direction that was different? Jesus tells the disciples in Matthew 28:19–20 that they are to baptize new converts and teach them "to obey everything I have commanded you." In the last chapter we examined some of Jesus's teachings, and in this chapter we discover that the church held to those same teachings and used them as foundational to their own. Thus discipleship for the church continues to follow the same pattern as discipleship in the Gospels.

The Church's Primary Discipleship Passages

To the Crowds
How to become a believer (disciple)—Matt. 28:19–20; Acts 2:14; 3:11–26

To the Believers (Disciples)
1. What believers do: they follow Jesus—1 Cor. 11:1; 1 Peter 2:21
2. What it means to follow Jesus:
   serving him—Acts 20:19; Rom.12:11; Col. 3:24; 1 Thess. 1:9
   serving others—1 Cor. 12:5; Eph. 4:12; 6:7; 1 Peter 4:10
3. How they follow Christ: they deny themselves and embrace his will for their lives—Rom. 6:1–14; 12:1; Gal. 2:20; Phil. 3:7–8
4. How they know they are following Christ:
   they believe and hold to his teaching—Acts 2:42; 6:1–7
   they love each other—1 John 3:14
   they bear fruit—Gal. 5:22; Col. 1:10
5. The result of following Christ: they, in turn, make disciples—Col. 4:3–4

The Church's Method of Discipleship

Now that we have discovered the church's disciple-making message, we turn to its disciple-making methodology. How did the early church make disciples?

Did they make disciples as Jesus did in the Gospels, or did the church go in a completely different direction?

When we looked at who made disciples in our study of disciple making in the Gospels, we found that it was one person. It was the master disciple maker—Jesus Christ. He was the one who took the disciples and others aside and discipled them. However, he was crucified, resurrected, and ascended to heaven, where he now occupies a position of authority at the right hand of the Father.

With Jesus no longer physically present, who is responsible to make disciples in the church? If you recall, I asked and answered this question in chapter 4, where I addressed the roles and responsibilities in disciple making. The answer was the Godhead, the individual, and the church. Each has a part or role in the disciple-making process. The Godhead plays a threefold role: the Father grows churches (1 Cor. 3:5–7), the Son builds churches (Matt. 16:18), and the Spirit transforms churches (2 Cor. 3:17–18). The individual disciple (believer) plays a role in the sense that he or she may or may not be open to being discipled. One must be a willing participant or it will not happen. Finally, the church plays a role that is addressed in Matthew 28:19–20. And it is this role of the church that I want to focus on in this chapter.

As we have discovered in earlier chapters, Jesus commissioned his church to make disciples in the Great Commission (Matt. 28:19–20; Mark 16:15; Luke 24:46–49; John 20:21; Acts 1:8). In a sense Jesus continues to make disciples but does so through his church. Initially he gave responsibility to his disciples, who as the apostles were the key leaders of the early church. Thus discipleship was both the mission and the very life of the church. It is not to be one of several programs of the church; it is *the program* of the church. All the activities and programs of the church work together to make disciples. It is not a ministry in which a few dedicated disciple makers work with a limited number of people who want to mature in their faith. It is a ministry of the church that seeks to make disciples of all its people. Michael Wilkins says, "The primary point for us to keep in mind is that discipling today is always undertaken as an outgrowth of the life of the church, whereas prior to Pentecost it occurred with Jesus personally."[1]

When the Church Made Disciples

There is much continuity between Jesus's message of disciple making in the Gospels and that of the church in Acts and the Epistles. The discontinuity is only in who made disciples—in the Gospels it was Jesus, and in the Epistles, the church made disciples.

In the last chapter I pointed out that in the Old Testament and in the Gospels, God's people did not have the permanent indwelling of the Holy Spirit. We can see, for example, in the book of Judges that the Spirit would come into the lives of people, such as various judges, to empower them to lead their people (see Judges 15:14), but it was not a permanent presence (see 16:20). Jesus said in John 14:17 that the Spirit was with Jesus's disciples and *would be* in them. This was how the Spirit worked in the lives of believers pre-Pentecost.

After Pentecost all this changed. In Acts 1:4 Jesus instructed the disciples not to leave Jerusalem but to wait for the Father's gift of the Holy Spirit. Then he explained in verse 8 that the Holy Spirit would come on them and supply the power they would need to be witnesses of his resurrection in Jerusalem, Judea, Samaria, and to the ends of the earth. Thus something changed at Pentecost—the Holy Spirit took up permanent residence in the lives of God's people, the church.

Why is this important? Jesus taught that at least six significant changes would take place regarding the Spirit's role in the life of a disciple after Pentecost.

1. In some way the Holy Spirit would indwell or reside with the disciples. Jesus says, "The world cannot accept him, because it neither sees him nor knows him. But you know him, for he lives with you and will be in you" (John 14:17).
2. The Holy Spirit would be with them permanently. In John 14:16 Jesus says, "And I will ask the Father, and he will give you another Counselor to be with you forever—the Spirit of truth."
3. The Spirit would enable the disciples to bear witness to the Savior. In John 15:26–27 Jesus says to them, "When the Counselor comes, whom I will send to you from the Father, the Spirit of truth, who goes out from the Father, he will testify about me. And you also must testify, for you have been with me from the beginning."
4. The Holy Spirit would help them bear persecution (John 16:1–7).
5. The Holy Spirit would guide them into all truth. In John 16:12–13 Jesus tells them, "I have much more to say to you, more than you can now bear. But when he, the Spirit of truth, comes, he will guide you into all truth. He will not speak on his own; he will speak only what he hears, and he will tell you what is yet to come." And he adds that the Spirit will glorify the Son by making his truth known to them (v. 14).
6. In Acts 1:8 Jesus told the disciples that when the Holy Spirit came on them, they would be permanently empowered for their ministries in the church.

The Ministry of the Holy Spirit

Pre-Pentecost	Post-Pentecost
With them	In them
Temporary indwelling	Permanent indwelling
Did not bear witness of Jesus	Will bear witness of Jesus
Did not help them bear persecution	Will help them bear persecution
Did not guide them into all truth	Will guide them into all truth
Temporary empowerment	Permanent empowerment

The Church's Disciple Making

The church's approach to making disciples differed from Jesus's approach in the Gospels when it came to whom was discipled and when. However, there is much continuity as to how both made disciples. For the church this involved a crowd (a large group meeting), house churches (medium-sized and small group meetings), and one-on-one relationships.

The Crowd

Jesus ministered to the crowd in a large-group setting throughout the Gospels. His mission was to make disciples or lead them to become disciples (believers). The church also ministered to the crowd in a large-group setting. Luke tells us in Acts 2:14, "Then Peter stood up with the Eleven, raised his voice and addressed the crowd." Peter spotted an opportunity for evangelism and took advantage of it. The results are found in verse 41, where Luke says that about three thousand Jews came to faith and were baptized. Luke makes other references to the crowd. In Acts 8:6 Philip proclaimed Christ to a crowd in Samaria. In Acts 13:44–45 Paul preached to a crowd in Antioch, and in 17:13 Paul preached the word of God to a crowd at Berea.

What was the size of these crowds? We know that in Acts 2 the crowd consisted of no fewer than three thousand people. Five thousand men responded to Peter's second sermon (4:4). And it is likely that the total number including women and children may have been ten to fifteen thousand people.

House Churches

The early church met predominantly in medium and small groups or house churches. Luke reports of the Jerusalem church: "They broke bread in their homes and ate together with glad and sincere hearts" (Acts 2:46). In Acts 8:3 he says, "But Saul began to destroy the church. Going from house to house, he dragged off men and women and put them in prison." In Acts 20:20 Paul reminds the elders who were pastors of the house churches in Ephesus: "You know that I have not hesitated to preach anything that would be helpful to you but have taught you publicly and from house to house."

According to the book of Acts, the first believers came together in the private homes of individuals, such as Mary the mother of John (12:12), Lydia (16:40), Priscilla and Aquila (18:26), as well as others. Twice Paul makes mention of the church that met in the house of Aquila and Priscilla (Rom. 16:3–5; 1 Cor. 16:19), and he speaks of a church that met in Nympha's house in Laodicea (Col. 4:15) and one at Philemon's house (Philem. 2). For almost three hundred years the disciples met in homes, not in facilities constructed specifically for church meetings. This did not change until Constantine erected the first church buildings (basilicas) in the fourth century.

What was the size of these house churches? Robert Banks, a former professor at Fuller Seminary in Pasadena, California, writes:

> The entertaining room in a moderately well-to-do household could hold around thirty people comfortably—perhaps half as many again in an emergency. The larger meeting in Troas, for example, was so large that Eutychus had to use the windowsill for a seat (Acts 20:9). A meeting of the "whole church" may have reached forty to forty-five people—if the meeting spilled over into the atrium then the number could have been even greater, though no more than double that size—but many meetings may well have been smaller. The average membership was around thirty to thirty-five people.[2]

Thus these house churches likely ranged in size from a medium-sized group of forty to fifty people to a small group of ten to thirty people.

One-on-One Relationships

It is possible that Barnabas discipled Paul one-on-one (Acts 9:26–28), though it is not clear, and he may have discipled John Mark (15:37). Paul may have discipled Silas according to Acts 15:40. A clearer example is that of Priscilla and Aquila, who invited Apollos into their home (where the church met) to explain to him the way of God more adequately (18:26). I noted that there is not much evidence in the Scriptures that Jesus spent a lot of time in any one-on-one relationships. The same is true of the church, or at least little is said about one-on-one discipling. We must remember, though, that an important hermeneutical principle is that simply because a practice is not mentioned in Scripture does not mean it did not happen. And it would seem from the possible examples in Acts that those who did the discipling thought and acted strategically, spending their time with those who were or would be key leaders in the church, such as Paul, Apollos, Silas, John Mark, and others.

Regardless, there are several ways that our churches could effectively minister to their people one-on-one. I made the point in chapter 4 that each Christian must take responsibility for his or her own spiritual growth as one of Christ's disciples. The church could complement and enhance this by providing mature believers as counselors or mentors who at the very least help new believers and members map out an initial, personal program tailor-made for their growth. This could take place as part of or subsequent to a new members class. The church might also have a group of these mature people who are regularly available to work for a limited period of time with anyone who is interested in maturing in the faith. And this could be regularly announced in the various services of the church. This would not only help individual members who are just beginning their spiritual growth development, but it would also give a wonderful opportunity of service for those in the church who are further along in their development. Willow Creek Community Church discovered that these more mature believers were some of the least satisfied people in the church because they were not being used to minister to others. And I suspect that their discovery is true of many in North American churches. I know of few churches that are practicing such one-on-one approaches using their more mature, but often dissatisfied, believers, and I do not understand why more are not offering discipleship help. One of my purposes for writing this book is to encourage the approach of using mature believers to disciple the less mature.

In summary, as we compare the church's methods of discipleship with those of Jesus, we see that they were very similar. Whether this was intentional is not clear, but there is continuity, not discontinuity, between the two. The church did not attempt to blaze new trails with its methodology, and this should be instructive when we consider the methodology we use in our churches.

The Church's Methods for Making Disciples

The church (Peter) preached to the crowds (large groups).

The church met in large houses (medium-sized groups).

The church met in smaller houses (small groups).

The church ministered one-on-one (individually).

Questions for Reflection and Discussion

1. Some believe that the church's message and practice of disciple making were different from those of Jesus. Do you agree or disagree? Why or why not?
2. Was the church's audience different from Jesus's audience? If so, how so? How would you explain this?
3. How would you explain the similarities between Jesus's discipleship teaching and that of the church? What do we learn from this? How might this teaching be incorporated into your church's disciple-making process?
4. What impact does the Holy Spirit's ministry have on disciple making? How important is he to the process? The disciples were different in Acts than in the Gospels. They were much bolder and stronger in their faith. Could the presence of the Holy Spirit be a possible explanation for the difference?
5. Why do you think there are so few examples of one-on-one discipleship in the Scriptures? What might this suggest about how and whom we disciple?

PART 2

THE PROCESS
for MAKING MATURE DISCIPLES

With Jesus's and the church's message and methods for making disciples in mind, you as a concerned leader in your church, whether a pastor, staff person, or teacher, are ready to design a clear strategy for making mature disciples. First, you will determine what a mature disciple would look like in your church context. This will explain why you do what you do—your church's primary ministries. Second, you will evaluate and work with your current primary ministries that are in place to make disciples. Third, you will develop a way to measure your progress in making disciples. Fourth, you will address how to staff your church to make disciples. Finally, you will discover how to develop a church budget to make this happen.

7

HOW WOULD WE KNOW A
MATURE DISCIPLE IF WE SAW ONE?

The Characteristics of a Mature Disciple

I have written the first six chapters to help prepare churches for developing a clear, biblical strategy for making disciples. To accomplish a biblical strategy, it is imperative that a church and its leaders understand both Jesus's and the church's message and methodology of discipleship. I have also answered the question, What is a disciple and how does a church make one? All this is critical to a disciple-making ministry in today's church. Now we are actually ready to construct a clear process or pathway for making mature disciples that is tailor-made for your church.

To understand fully our goal—to produce a clear process for making mature believers in the church—we must clearly understand two key terms: *process* and *mature*. The first is *process* (and any of its synonyms—*strategy, pathway, path*, and others). The goal is to design a *process* to move people from where they are spiritually (a nonbeliever or immature believer) to maturity. Process consists of your primary ministries, those that you believe are essential to bring people to maturity in Christ. Determining what these should be is the goal of the next chapter.

Our ultimate goal is to develop not just disciples (believers) but *mature* disciples. To accomplish this, we must determine the characteristics or marks of a mature disciple, which is the goal of this chapter. First, we will examine a tool entitled the Spiritual Journey Evaluation and then address the characteristics of a mature disciple.

The Spiritual Journey Evaluation

Several years ago, Bob Gilliam developed an evaluation that provides us with a necessary introduction to this chapter and those that follow, along with several important benchmarks.

We discovered in chapter 4 that the church is responsible to assist its people in becoming and then growing as Jesus's disciples. We also found out in chapter 2 that currently in Europe and North America the church is not doing very well at this. So we must pause and ask why. Why are most churches not making disciples?

Bob Gilliam affirms the failure of the church to make disciples and then gets at some of the key elements that explain why this is the case. In 1994 Gilliam developed the Spiritual Journey Evaluation as an attempt to determine if today's church is making disciples. The evaluation consisted of a survey given to nearly four thousand attenders in thirty-five churches in several denominations scattered from Florida to Washington. After analyzing the results, Gilliam observed, "Most people in these churches are not growing spiritually. Of those taking this survey, 24 percent indicated that their behavior was sliding backward and 41 percent said they were 'static' in their spiritual growth."[1] Therefore, 65 percent of those responding indicated that they were either plateaued or declining in their spiritual growth. If you recall, I presented this information in chapter 2 on how the church is doing, but I did not present the following.

What does all this mean? The answer forms the basis for this chapter and the next and provides you with some disciple-making benchmarks. Gilliam continues:

> It seems clear from all this data that for some reason churches aren't effectively being intentional about making disciples. The churches provided as examples aren't exceptions but are normative compared to the experience of most. There is very little reason to believe that your church is any different. Why? Their leaders don't know what a disciple looks like. They don't know how to make a disciple even if they can define one. They don't know how church programs work together to make disciples. They have no way to measure progress. Their leaders aren't model disciples but they do reproduce after their kind. They don't know how to become intentional without splitting the church.[2]

Not much has changed for the church since Gilliam conducted his survey. Perhaps things have gotten worse. Gilliam focused our attention on six reasons for this failure.

1. "Their leaders don't know what a disciple looks like." To develop a clear strategy, your congregation must know what a disciple looks like. You must answer the question, What are the marks of an authentic Christian? I will address this in the rest of this chapter.
2. "They don't know how to make a disciple even if they can define one." As mentioned earlier in this book, my experience as a seminary professor and church consultant is that most people cannot define a disciple. Gilliam is correct when he states that most churches do not know how to make disciples. The provocative question is, Where would a church or its pastors learn how to make disciples? I will address this issue in the next chapter.
3. "They don't know how church programs work together to make disciples." All churches have programs. My experience is that few churches have thought through what these programs should be and how they should work together to make disciples. This will also be a goal of the next chapter.
4. "They have no way to measure progress." The way to measure progress is to have in place a formal system of evaluation. Since people evaluate all churches informally, I would argue that the church should design a formal evaluation process and thus benefit from it. But how might a church develop such a system? I will address this in chapter 9.
5. "Their leaders aren't model disciples but they do reproduce after their kind." Fortunately this is not true of many leaders in our churches. Still, most of us have recognized a moral decline of church leadership in general and staff in particular in the latter half of the twentieth and into the twenty-first century. I will address this moral decline in chapter 10.
6. "They don't know how to become intentional without splitting the church." While this section of the book addresses this topic indirectly, it is the goal of this book to help you implement an intentional pathway for making mature disciples that unites rather than splits a church.

The Characteristics of a Mature Disciple

The goal of a church's ministry is to bring its people to spiritual maturity, which, theologically, is the ultimate goal of the Great Commission. Therefore an important question that a church must answer is, What does spiritual maturity look like? Gilliam notes above that a major part of the problem is that churches do not know what a disciple looks like. How would we know a mature disciple if he or she were to walk through the door? We must discover the marks of a mature believer, and that can be done with the following three-step process.

Step 1: Determine the Church's Mission

To discover the marks of a mature believer, we must return to the church's mission. The church's disciple-making process is inextricably tied to its mission. The process is the strategy that ultimately accomplishes the mission in the life of the church. To jump into the disciple-making process without determining the church's mission is to get the proverbial cart in front of the horse. As we discovered earlier, the church's mission has always been and will continue to be the Great Commission. I advise all churches to develop a mission statement for their church. It is to be short and memorable so that everyone in the church will know what it is and be able to articulate it when asked to identify it. Some examples are "To turn irreligious people into fully devoted followers of Christ"; "To present Christ as Savior and pursue Christ as Lord"; "To know Christ and make him known." At the heart of each of these mission statements is the Great Commission.

From a discipleship perspective, the church's mission involves both making disciples (evangelism) and maturing them (edification). To picture this, we need to return to and review the Disciple-Making Continuum that I introduced in chapter 1. Before a person comes to faith, he or she is in what I refer to optimistically as the prebirth stage. Prebirth is the time one is an unbeliever. At a point in time a person hears the gospel and accepts Christ as Savior and experiences a new birth (John 3:1–8). Thus this new believer has passed from prebirth to new birth. However, the new believer is not to stop at that point. There is more to Christianity than excellent fire insurance. From this point on, the converted believer is to begin the process of spiritual growth toward maturity (see Phil. 3:15; Col. 1:28–29; Heb. 5:11–6:3). I believe that there are degrees of maturity and at some point a believer crosses a point where he or she enters the early stages of maturity and hopefully continues to grow and mature as a disciple.

Disciple-Making Continuum

Nondisciple	New Disciple	Growing Disciple
Prebirth (unbelief)	New birth (belief)	Maturity (growth)

The Marks of a Mature Disciple

Step 1: Determine the church's mission.

Step 2: Ask the Sanctification Question

After the church has articulated the Great Commission in a short, memorable statement, determining that its mission is to win people to Christ and help them mature as believers, we must decide what characteristics a maturing believer would exhibit. To do this we must ask the sanctification question.

I suggest that a group of leaders brainstorm, based on your knowledge of the New Testament, to come up with a list of characteristics. You need to begin with a descriptive list, such as the following: baptism, worship, prayer, evangelism, a knowledge and application of Scripture, service, communion (the Lord's Supper), fellowship, the fruit of the Spirit, financial giving, fruit bearing (general good works), love, fear of God, and so on. And some would include various spiritual disciplines, some of which are included in this list.

Next, synthesize all the biblical characteristics under at least two but not more than five headings. This is a theological exercise. Some specific characteristics can be combined under other broader ones. For example, from a theological perspective, you could put prayer, the Lord's Supper, financial giving, and other components of worship under worship. (Scott Horrell, a friend and colleague at Dallas Seminary, has written on this topic and in a private conversation told me that he places service under worship as well.) One church that I worked with, Fellowship Bible Church in Dallas, Texas, puts all the characteristics under three Cs:

1. Celebrate (worship)
2. Connect (biblical instruction and fellowship)
3. Contribute (evangelism and service)

While I really like the three Cs, I prefer to place the characteristics under the five functions of the church. (Note that these five are similar to but not quite the same as Rick Warren's five purposes for the church.) The five functions are the following:

1. Worship (Acts 2:42–43, 46–47)
2. Fellowship or community (Acts 2:42, 44–46)
3. Biblical instruction (Acts 2:42)
4. Evangelism (Acts 2:41, 47)
5. Service (Acts 2:44–45)

Worship of God is the first characteristic of a maturing believer and involves up-reach. When we worship God, we are attributing supreme worth to him. And Jesus tells us that God seeks our worship, "Yet a time is coming and has now come when the true worshipers will worship the Father in spirit and truth, for they are the kind of worshipers the Father seeks" (John 4:23).

Fellowship involves in-reach. We need to be involved with other believers as they are part of the church, and we desperately need one another, as we discovered through the one-another passages in chapter 4. I have found that I experience the greatest doubts about my faith when I do not find time in my busy schedule to be with other believers. So a maturing disciple will spend time in fellowship with other believers.

Biblical instruction involves in-reach. We believers need to know and apply God's Word to our lives. The writer of Hebrews warns that one reason some believers remain immature in their faith is a lack of knowledge and application of Scripture in their lives (Heb. 5:11–6:3). According to Willow Creek Community Church's congregational survey, 60 percent of their most mature people in the church want "more in-depth Bible teaching."[3] A maturing disciple studies God's Word and follows its teachings.

Evangelism involves outreach. God wants us to share our faith with those who do not know Christ as Savior (Col. 4:3–6). My consulting ministry has shown me that few churches from coast-to-coast and border-to-border in America value evangelism. Consequently it is not being done. This is an area where the church really needs to turn up the heat. A maturing disciple will find opportunities to share his or her faith with unbelievers.

Service is in-reach. God has given every believer a spiritual gift to use in ministry (1 Peter 4:10–11). This is critical in the life of the church. Paul teaches in Ephesians 4:12–13 that service is necessary if a church is to mature in Christ. In the Willow Creek Community Church congregational survey, they discovered that their more mature believers were strongest on service as an expression of their faith. Thus they believe that the church's primary role in the lives of their most mature believers is to provide them with serving opportunities.[4]

Another way to group the characteristics would be to use the three marks of a disciple, given in John's Gospel. They are the following:

1. Abiding in God's Word (John 8:31–32)
2. Loving one another (John 13:34–35)
3. Bearing fruit (John 15:8)

While I covered these briefly in chapter 5, I want to revisit them with a little more detail. In both John's Gospel and especially his letters, he wrestles with how one can know that he or she is a believer. In 1 John, for example, he provides a number of tests for a person to take that are designed to answer this question. So we should not be surprised to see him doing much the same in his Gospel in chapters 8, 13, and 15.

In John 8:31–32 Jesus speaks to believing Jews, and he tells them that they are really his disciples (believers) if they hold to his teaching. I believe that he is saying they are believers if they agree with his teaching and do not abandon or fall away from it in the future. Disagreement and abandonment are signs of unbelief. The result of holding to his teaching is knowing truth and freedom. When I read this passage, I am reminded of Matthew 28:20, where Jesus tells the Eleven that they are to teach their disciples to obey everything he has commanded of them.

Jesus's teaching in John 13:34–35 is fairly straightforward. He tells the disciples that the mark of a disciple (believer) is love for one another, and he uses his love for them as an example of what that love looks like. Jesus repeats this later in the form of a command in John 15:17. This love for one another is also one of the tests of faith in 1 John 3:14–15.

Finally, Jesus's teaching on fruit bearing in John 15:1–17 is not as explicit. In verse 8 he teaches his disciples: "This is to my Father's glory, that you bear much fruit, showing yourselves to be my disciples." The problem is pinning down what he meant by bearing fruit. The term *fruit* is mentioned eight times in this chapter in a progression from "fruit" (v. 2) to "more fruitful" (v. 2) to "much fruit" (vv. 5, 8). The question is, what is the fruit that he is talking about? The context does not answer the question. Likely it is general fruit bearing that involves a lifestyle characterized by good works befitting a true disciple. This is borne out by the fire figure in verse 6 and the broader context of the Gospels, as in Matthew 7:15–20, where the Savior teaches:

> Watch out for false prophets. They come to you in sheep's clothing, but inwardly they are ferocious wolves. By their fruit you will recognize them. Do people pick grapes from thornbushes, or figs from thistles? Likewise every good tree bears good fruit, but a bad tree bears bad fruit. A good tree cannot bear bad fruit, and a bad tree cannot bear good fruit. Every tree that does not bear good fruit is cut down and thrown into the fire. Thus, by their fruit you will recognize them.

One function that some might argue is missing from these three marks of a disciple is worship. While John does not state that worship is a mark of a true disciple—at least not in the same way as he emphasizes abiding in God's Word, loving each other, and bearing fruit—he does say in John 4:24 to a Samaritan woman: "God is spirit, and his worshipers must worship in spirit and in truth."

In *Following the Master* Michael Wilkins notes the early practices of the church in Acts 2:42: the apostles' teaching, fellowship, breaking of bread, and prayer. He explains, "We find in these practices of the early church—devoted to the apostles' teaching, fellowship, breaking of bread, and prayer—the four essential elements in the religious practice of the Christian church. . . . We see here the essential ingredients of the way in which the new community sustained their life of fellowship."[5] Thus you might want to use these four practices as your marks for a maturing disciple. However, later Wilkins seems to expand this list when he says, "We may go so far as to say that in many ways discipleship is the overall goal of the church, including evangelism, nurturing, fellowship, leadership, worship, etc."[6]

So give some thought to the characteristics you believe are part of a mature disciple.

The Marks of a Mature Disciple

Step 1: Determine the church's mission.
Step 2: Ask the sanctification question.

Step 3: Ask the Communication Question

The communication question asks, How will you communicate these characteristics or marks so that the congregation knows them and, most important, remembers them? First, when you synthesize all the biblical characteristics under not more than five categories, you aid the communication process. People tend not to remember more than five points and may even struggle with that many. So developing the characteristics is not only a theological exercise but a communication one as well.

Second, determine which of the following will best communicate your characteristics to your people: alliteration, an acrostic, a person, an object, pictures, symbols, or some other form. The only limit to the form is your creativity and imagination.

See if any of the following examples would work for your church.

ALLITERATION

Alliteration involves choosing terms that all begin with the same letter. For example, at the last church I pastored, we came up with the four Cs. Here is how we communicated them. We placed our mission statement that identified a mature believer as a fully functioning follower of Christ at the top and followed it with the four Cs:

> Our mission is to help our people become fully functioning followers of Christ. Fully functioning followers have four characteristics:
>
> 1. Conversion—they are converted and know Christ as Savior.
> 2. Community—they value and are part of a biblically functioning community (small group).
> 3. Commitment—they have made the deepest of commitments of their lives to Christ.
> 4. Contribution—they are contributing to Christ's kingdom and the church by serving people, supporting the church financially, and sharing their faith (the three Ss).

If I were to produce this again, I would add a fifth C—celebration. Somehow we left out celebration or worship.

The church I attend (Lake Pointe Church in Rockwall, Texas) has developed the following mission and characteristics using four Ws:

> Our mission is to share Christ and build believers. Believers display four marks:
>
> 1. Worship—they worship God both corporately and privately.
> 2. Word—they live by God's Word, understanding that it is the authority for all of life.

3. Work—they contribute to God's work by using their gifts to serve the body, to give financially, and to relate experientially.

4. World—they impact the world by reaching out to their unchurched, lost friends and becoming personally involved in world missions.

Willow Creek Community Church has the following mission and characteristics:

> Our mission is to turn irreligious people into fully devoted followers of Christ. Fully devoted followers of Christ have five characteristics: grace, growth, gifts, groups, and good stewardship.

If someone were to plant a church, an option would be to use terms beginning with E: evangelism, encouragement (fellowship), exaltation (worship), equipping (biblical instruction), and enlisting (service).

An Acrostic

Some churches use an acrostic to communicate the characteristics of a mature disciple. The first letters of the characteristics when combined spell out a memorable word that could tie back into the mission statement. For example, below is the mission statement and characteristics of Valleydale Baptist Church in Birmingham, Alabama. Their acrostic forms the word *grace*, which is memorable for their congregation. Note also that Valleydale uses strong action verbs rather than nouns.

> Our mission is to provide the best opportunity for people to become fully devoted Christ followers. Fully devoted Christ followers have five characteristics:
>
> Glorify God through meaningful worship.
> Relate together in biblical community.
> Apply God's truth through discipleship.
> Cultivate a lifestyle of service.
> Expand God's kingdom through evangelism.

Grace Brethren Church of Wooster, Ohio, uses the same acrostic because it matches their name and each characteristic also represents its core values.

> Our mission is to develop all people into fully devoted Christ followers. Fully devoted Christ followers have five characteristics. They desire to:
>
> Grow
> Reach out
> Act
> Connect
> Exalt

The advantage for this church is that if its members can remember the name of their church, they can remember the characteristics of a mature disciple. And the same goes for their core values.

The Bandera Road Community Church in San Antonio, Texas, has developed as their acrostic the word *fitness*, tying it back into their mission statement.

> Our mission is to lead people that are far from God to be spiritually fit followers of Christ. Spiritually fit followers of Christ have seven characteristics:

> > Family ties (community)
> > Intimacy with God
> > Treasure (stewardship)
> > Networked (mobilized)
> > Engaging the lost
> > Spiritual practices
> > Social action

As you develop an acrostic, it is important to make it truly memorable. Again, when you have more than six characteristics, people may remember the first letters but not the words or what they represent. The way to know is ask people. Quiz them and see if they remember the characteristics.

A DIAGRAM

Create a diagram to illustrate the characteristics of a mature disciple. You could use the heart, head, hands, and feet of the human body to communicate your characteristics. You could also combine this with alliteration. For example, *word* (2 Tim. 3:15) goes with the head (Matt. 22:37); *worship* (Rom. 12:1; John 4:24) with the heart (Ps. 24:4; Matt. 22:37); *work* (Eph. 2:10) with the hands (Ps. 24:4); and *witness* with the feet (Rom. 10:15). I developed this in consultation with Neptune Baptist Church, located near Jacksonville, Florida.

These are just a few ways to communicate your characteristics of maturity to your people. Be creative and come up with your own. To some people, using one of these methods may seem gimmicky. If this is a problem, you may want to consider another approach. However, the advantages of these communication tools clearly outweigh any disadvantages.

The Marks of a Mature Disciple

Step 1: Determine the church's mission—the Great Commission (Matt. 28:19–20).

Step 2: Ask the sanctification question—What are the marks or characteristics of a mature disciple?

Step 3: Ask the communication question—How will we communicate the marks to the congregation?

Questions for Reflection and Discussion

1. Do you believe that the ultimate goal of the local church is spiritual maturity? Why or why not? What Scripture would support this position?
2. Do you agree that the mission of every church is the Great Commission? Why or why not? What is the mission of your church? If it is not the Great Commission, then what is it (do not fudge on this one)?
3. Does your church have a mission statement? If not, why not? If so, what is it? Is it short and memorable? Does it have the Great Commission at its core?
4. What are some biblical characteristics of a mature disciple? Did you come up with some that the author did not? If so, what are they?
5. In communicating your characteristics, do you prefer alliteration, an acrostic, a diagram, or some other approach? What method would you use?
6. This chapter provides you with several churches' characteristics. Which do you like best? Would the way the church communicates them work for your church? Why or why not? If not, you will need to design a vehicle of your own. What might that be?
7. Is the name of your church short enough that you could use it as an acrostic for your characteristics? Would this work as well for your core values?

8

How Do Churches
Make Mature Disciples?

The Church's Ministries for Discipleship

We learned in chapter 7 that the church needs to determine its characteristics of spiritual maturity and a way to clearly communicate them to the congregation so that its people know and remember them. The next step is to design a process or strategy that will help people incarnate the characteristics. This is the sanctification or spiritual transformation process that leads to maturity and involves the church's ministries. It is your ministries and their sequencing that make up your disciple-making pathway or game plan. If a visitor or a member asked you how your church would help him or her grow as a disciple, what would your answer be? My goal in this chapter is to help you answer this question by designing a disciple-making pathway for your church. To accomplish this we will identify and explore your primary disciple-making ministries.

Church Ministries

The church's ministries are its means or activities that God uses to implement or incarnate its marks of maturity in the believer's life. The ministry involves not only the activities (what we do) but the staff (who does it) and the budget (how much it costs to operate it). In this chapter I will address the activities of ministries, and I will address staffing and budgeting in chapters 10 and 11.

I use the term *ministries* (and on occasion *activities*) as a broad term that includes various services, group meetings, events, seminars, programs, personal relationships, and so forth.

If I were to attend your church one Sunday unannounced and visit a Sunday school class or a small group and ask those in attendance why they are in the class or group, what would they say? I suspect that at first there would be silence. Then, if it is a Sunday school class, someone might raise a hand and answer, "To study the Bible." Then I would ask, "Why study the Bible?" Someone has said that if you ask why often enough you will get to the heart of the matter. What I am attempting to learn is whether or not the class or group, or any ministry for that matter, understands its purpose or why it is doing what it is doing.

Every ministry must have a clearly articulated purpose or end that answers the question, why are we doing what we are doing? Every ministry housed under the roof of the church and any beyond must answer this question. Nothing should be done for its own sake. For example, we do not implement a small-group ministry merely to say we have one or that we are on the cutting edge. That makes no sense. If one of your ministries is a Sunday school program or a small-group ministry, then it must have a clearly understood and well-articulated purpose (and some may have more than one). And that purpose must in some way lead back to and contribute to the church's mission, which is to see its people grow to spiritual maturity. For example, a small-group ministry is the means to provide your people with fellowship and a sense of community, which is vital to making disciples and moving toward spiritual maturity. If a church sponsors a ministry that has no purpose and therefore does not contribute to the mission and maturity, then someone needs to explain why the ministry was started and, more importantly, why it should continue, outside of the fact that those involved in it will get mad if it is discontinued.

It is also important to note that God has entrusted us with the responsibility of crafting the ministries or means that will accomplish his ends. In effect, under God's direction, we are selecting activities for the Holy Spirit to use in the life of the church. Thus we must take this process very seriously. In all humility, we are asking God to take these ministry activities and use them as a means to accomplish his ends—to grow his church (1 Cor. 3:5–9). This should be a most humbling experience, and we should never take it lightly.

Bill Hybels, pastor of Willow Creek Community Church, underlines the importance of our ministry means for making authentic disciples:

> Other churches may take a different approach; they have a different thumbprint. And that's fine. But every church needs to grapple with the question of how to follow the specific instructions that Jesus gave all of us: "Therefore go and

make disciples of all nations, baptizing them in the name of the Father and of the Son and of the Holy Spirit, and teaching them to obey everything I have commanded you."

It's not enough to have a succinct mission statement engraved on a plaque and hung in the hallway where it can inspire everyone. While that's a good step, it's only wishful thinking unless there's a concrete, Spirit-inspired game plan to turn it into reality.[1]

And it is your church's primary ministries that are vital to your disciple-making game plan. You design and implement these ministries to make and mature disciples.

Before I go any further, I must include a disclaimer. Just because a church has a ministry game plan does not guarantee disciples. While the church's leadership does its best under God's guidance to develop its ministries, there is no guarantee that its people will actively, willfully pursue them. Some people could be involved in all of the church's primary ministries but be merely going through the motions and not maturing. They are "checklist people" who go through life completing checklists, and the church's primary ministries become simply another checklist to make them feel as if they have accomplished something each weekend for God. Dan Kimball, an emergent church pastor, wisely warns: "A numbered, step-by-step prescription for spiritual progress many times can prohibit organic growth."[2]

Types of Ministries

There are numerous ministries that take place in churches all over the world, and all of them fall under one of two headings—primary or secondary ministries.

Primary Ministries

IMPORTANCE

The primary ministries are the most important in helping your congregation embrace the marks of a disciple and move toward maturity. They are not ministry electives but ministry essentials. They provide the blueprint or game plan to accomplish the church's mission and are mandatory for those who are serious about spiritual growth. These ministries are designed for and thus benefit all believers in the church, and it is expected that every believer will involve him- or herself in these ministries. Thus the church will need repeatedly to communicate their importance to the congregation. If you are a pastor, you may get tired of hearing yourself repeat this to the congregation, and you may be convinced that they are tired of hearing about it as well. Some sage has said, though, that when you get to this point, the congregation is just beginning to get the message.

ASSIMILATION PROCESS

As I am using the term in this book, *assimilation* addresses how a church orders or arranges its primary ministries to bring people into the life of the church, keep them involved in that life, and move them on to spiritual maturity. It relates to how your church moves people from outside the life of the church to become a vital part of that life. When a person desires to connect with your church, how does he or she do so? What activities, events, or relationships would he or she experience first, second, third, and so on? How have you arranged these ministries to help a person come to faith and then move on to maturity? The answer reveals your assimilation process.

THE NUMBER OF PRIMARY MINISTRIES

Each church is different. It is possible for a church to have only one primary event, especially if it is small. Most have at least two primary events and some have as many as seven. Following are several examples of the number of primary ministries, moving from the typical traditional church to the emergent church (that people of the younger generations, such as Mark Driscoll in Seattle, Washington, are currently planting all across North America). In addition to the number of such ministries, this section will also provide you with several samples of other church's primary ministries that could prove helpful as you design yours.

For many years, the typical traditional church has offered three events that make up what some of us refer to as the "three to thrive" strategy. The first is the Sunday morning event that consists of a Sunday school class followed by a large-group meeting for worship and the preaching of God's Word. The second is a Sunday evening event that most often involves a second sermon or Bible study led by the pastor. In a larger church, a staff person or an intern may have opportunity to preach during this service. In addition, some churches have a ministry for the young people and children, such as a training union or an Awana program. The third event is the Wednesday evening prayer meeting. Some use this as a time of prayer, but others may use it as another preaching or teaching event. I so enjoyed teaching the Bible that in one of my churches I used most of the time on Wednesday night to teach and reserved the last ten minutes or so for prayer requests and prayer.

When we examine today's contemporary churches, we find a broad range of primary ministry events.

Some congregations in the Fellowship Bible Church movement have a large-group worship and preaching event and small groups. The large-group event is the Sunday morning worship celebration, where people present themselves corporately to God, study his Word, apply truth, and respond in various ways to God's greatness. The small groups, or Community Groups, involve from eight to sixteen adults who join one another on their faith journey, encourage one another to put their faith in action, pray together, may play together (enjoy one another's company), and have opportunity to meet the needs of others in the group or in the broader church through sacrificial acts of service.

The church that has the most ministry events that I am aware of is Willow Creek Community Church. They have seven primary activities or ministries. Hybels explains, "The strategy we pursued for many years took shape when I wrote it down one day on a napkin in California. Every believer at Willow Creek sees it as their blueprint to accomplish our mission. We call it our seven-step strategy and it's part of our 'thumbprint' as a church."[3]

In assimilation order they are the following:

1. Build an authentic relationship with a nonbeliever.
2. Share a verbal witness.
3. Bring the seeker to a service designed especially for him or her.
4. Regularly attend a believer's service.
5. Join a small group.
6. Discover, develop, and deploy one's spiritual gifts.
7. Steward one's resources in a God-honoring way.[4]

Saddleback Valley Community Church, pastored by Rick Warren in Southern California, has four ministry events with an optional fifth event for leaders. In assimilation order, they are:

1. Bridge events that are community-wide events designed to connect with their community and make it aware of the church.
2. A weekend seeker service—much like that of Willow Creek—where members can bring their unsaved friends to whom they are witnessing.
3. Small groups that provide fellowship, personal care, and a sense of belonging.
4. A Life Development Institute that provides opportunities for spiritual growth, such as Bible studies, seminars, workshops, and mentoring opportunities.
5. An optional SALT ministry (Saddleback Advanced Leadership Training) for the training of leaders.[5]

As I consult with churches, I encourage them to embrace fewer primary ministries, not more. The reason is "less is more." The average congregant will not remember five to seven primary ministries. Opting for fewer ministries promotes clarity and encourages the leadership to "do less" well.

My friend Jeff Gilmore is the pastor of Parkview Evangelical Free Church in Iowa City, Iowa. He has taken a slightly different approach. The church offers four primary disciple-making ministries: worship, small groups, an ABF (Adult Bible Fellowship), and a class for congregational mobilization (people attend this only once, so it is not ongoing for those who have been through it). While they offer small-group ministries and ABFs, they ask their people to choose which best fits their discipleship needs. This gives their people some leeway in pursuing discipleship. For this to work, the church has to communicate regularly and well these two options and their unique benefits.

The new kid on the block is the emergent church that consists mostly of the younger Bridger generation or Millennials. An interesting characteristic of this group is their thumbs-down attitude toward structure and organization. Someone shared with me recently that he was at a meeting of emergent church leaders, and they decided that they wanted to move in a particular direction (I cannot recall what that was). So they began to organize to accomplish their goal. What was humorous was that someone raised his hand and pointed out to the group that they were doing the very thing they were against, and everyone laughed. They realized that the accomplishment of their goal required organization and structure.

I believe that most new church plants develop and organize ministries similar to the way that churches have been organized in the past. Some have a large-group time of worship because of their size. And most have small-group ministries. Some with which I have connected focus primarily on the small group, which may meet in a house as a house church. And they attempt to address the biblical ministry functions in that setting. As they grow numerically, they will start other house churches, and in time some will gather once a month for a large-group worship event. But clearly the emphasis is on the small-group ministry. Consequently their primary ministries may be very similar to those of the Fellowship Bible churches. However, the small-group ministry is the first and the primary point of assimilation, whereas the worship-preaching service is second.

As the emergent churches grow and develop, they will react to what they see as the inadequacies of the Builder and Boomer church ministries. The Boomer churches did the same to the Builder churches. I believe this is most healthy. Dan Kimball instructs, "Emerging church leaders need to rethink the whole concept of discipleship, because quite frankly, if we're honest, the modern church hasn't done that good a job. If making disciples is our primary goal, we'd better not be afraid to reconsider how we go about it."[6]

Ultimately a determining factor in addressing how many primary ministries you might include in your maturity process is your culture. We must ask, How many meetings should we expect our people to attend? Given the busyness of our current culture, how much time should we ask them to give to the church? Many typical, traditional churches established during the era of the Builder generation asked their people to attend three primary meetings a week. Today many churches find that their people attend less. For example, one large, thriving mega–Bible church in the Dallas area surveyed its people and found that most attend once every three weeks. So what are your expectations for your congregation?

The Purpose of the Primary Ministries

Regardless of the number of events a church offers, the idea is for people to move into the life of the church, embracing all its primary ministries, whether as few as two or as many as Willow's seven. This is most important. Again, these are not discipleship electives but essentials. So if the first assimilation ministry is the large-group time of worship, then most will begin there. But they must not stop or cluster there, as so many tend to do. The challenge is to move people to the next ministry event—to get them out of the stands and onto the discipleship playing field so they attend not only the worship service but a small group or Sunday school or both as well. And the process continues for any other primary ministries.

Thus if you have three primary ministries, the goal and challenge is to involve all your people in all three ministries. Embracing these disciple-making ministries signals an individual disciple's growing commitment to the Savior and the church. It will also help the church evaluate how well it is making disciples. Simply count and regularly keep track of how many people are involved in these ministries. Is the number growing or decreasing? I will say more about evaluation in the next chapter.

Age Groups

Every church is made up of people from various age groups—adults, youth, and children. I recommend that all of your church's age groups follow the same disciple-making process. Initially, you plan for the entire church with the focus on adults, and the disciple-making ministries you choose for them will be much the same as or similar to those for youth and children. For example, if you decide to have a large-group worship time, a Sunday school class, and a small group for the adults, you could do the same for the youth and children. Obviously in smaller churches some of the ministries will be the same as those for adults, youth, and children. For example, due to the church's size, the youth and children participate in the adult worship experience but have their own age-specific classes and/or groups.

Secondary Ministries

All ministries beyond the primary ones are the secondary ministries. As a consultant, one way I help churches identify their secondary ministries is to list all of their ministries on a large whiteboard. Next we circle the few primary ministries, and those that are left are the secondary ministries.

Importance

Secondary ministries are secondary in the sense that they are not essential to the church's purpose of making mature disciples. They are electives, not essentials, so they are not as important to the church's disciple-making strategy as the primary ministries. Still, when combined with the primary ministries, they provide an overall picture of how all the church's ministries are operating in light of the church's disciple-making process. Examples of secondary ministries are men's and women's Bible studies, vacation Bible school, the midweek service, special Easter or Christmas programs, a Christian day school, twelve-step ministries, Mother's Day Out, homeschooling groups, and so on.

THE ORIGIN OF THE SECONDARY MINISTRIES

Secondary ministries have likely come into existence because the church may not have done a good job with a primary ministry in the past. It may have gone through several years with a poor preacher and/or poor worship. Or the Sunday school program may not have taught the Scriptures well, and people felt they needed more in-depth teaching. Thus, for example, the women or men decided to start a men's or women's Bible study.

THE PROBLEM

There are at least five problems with secondary ministries.[7]

1. *Distraction not attraction.* Many of the Builder churches have added numerous secondary ministries, thinking that if they offer more programs, they will attract more people. Some even pride themselves in their many programs. I refer to this as the "menu philosophy of ministry." We have learned, however, that people more than programs attract people. A plethora of programs will attract some people, but not to the degree that many used to think it would. Instead, many programs distract people from the primary disciple-making ministries.

2. *Confusion not clarity.* These ministries cause confusion for the congregation. For example, when I go out to eat at a restaurant, I prefer fewer choices. When I open the menu and I see numerous entrées, I find it confusing and more difficult to decide because I like everything I see on the menu. They all look so good. When people look at numerous ministry opportunities, many look good, and they are confused. We must opt for clarity over confusion, and this happens when we limit or even eliminate secondary ministries, not mixing them in with the primary ones. People need to know what is expected of them in terms of the church's ministries. That is clarity.

3. *Complexity not simplicity.* People are not dumb. Nevertheless, the KISS principle (Keep it simple, Simon) is always the better route. Why make ministry matters complex when we can make them simple? Simple wins out every time. In addition, we have a saying at the Malphurs Group that "less is more." Simplicity always involves less, while complexity involves more.

4. *Diffusing energy instead of directing energy.* People expend energy when involved in the various ministries of the church, and that energy can

be either diffused or directed. It is the difference between a laser and a lightbulb. A laser directs or focuses energy, and this is what needs to happen with the primary ministries. All of our energy is to be focused on them, and people must focus on them if they are to become growing disciples. A lightbulb diffuses energy. And the secondary ministries do the same. They add to the ministries list and thus diffuse or distract energy away from the essentials.

5. *Requiring staff and funding instead of freeing staff and funding.* Some secondary ministries require the involvement of staff and funds that the church would better spend on the primary ministries. We will see in the last two chapters that a church must both staff and budget around the essential primary disciple-making ministries not the elective nonessentials.

So what can the church with a rather sizeable "ministry menu" do? I have at least three suggestions.

1. Some ministries can be eliminated. The way to accomplish this is through evaluation. It is imperative that churches evaluate not only their people who are involved in ministry (both lay and staff) but their ministries. Regardless of how you discontinue these ministries, be aware that when you start eliminating them, those who have been part of them will be upset with you. So make sure you communicate with these people. They need to know why you are eliminating some of their favorite ministries. And be prepared even to lose some of them from the church.

2. Make it difficult to start new ministries. Keep the ministry menu lean. New secondary ministries must demonstrate a strong need for their existence, must have an in-house trained leader, must not require the services of the staff, must not depend on the budget for funding, must not attempt to raise funds from the congregation, and the leaders must be involved in the church's leadership development program.

3. Tie some of the secondary ministries into the primary ones. For example, vacation Bible school could become a regular part of the church's primary evangelism strategy. A women's Bible study could become an extension of the Sunday school ministry, and the same with a men's Bible study. When you do this, you will need to communicate this constantly to your people. It is important that they connect what may have been a secondary ministry to the primary ministry, or the secondary ministry could become more important for some than the primary ministry. And they must be encouraged not to abandon a primary ministry for a secondary one. Secondary ministries are to augment not distract from a primary ministry. The point here is that some former secondary ministries can supplement the primary ministries and enhance spiritual maturity. However, I would still be reluctant to assign staff and funding to these ministries.

Designing a Unique Disciple-Making Strategy

Unless yours is a church plant, designing a disciple-making and maturing process will largely involve critiquing your current process in general and your primary ministries in particular. But how does it work? The following three steps will show the way.

Step 1: Construct a Maturity Matrix

The Maturity Matrix consists of a horizontal and a vertical axis as represented in the figure below. (I have also included a blank sample in appendix C for your use.) Here we are using the matrix to help you design your strategy to make disciples. It will also help you to evaluate your process and explain and communicate it to your congregation in the future. In chapter 7 you identified at least two but not more than five characteristics of a mature believer. Place them along the top of the horizontal axis, as I have done with the five Cs in the figure on page 97 (I have included in parentheses a function under each C for instructional purposes. It is not necessary for you to do this).

Step 2: Identify Your Primary Ministries

Next, write all of your church ministries on a pad (or whiteboard if working with a team). Identify your current primary ministries (at least two but not more than seven), and place them along the vertical axis in assimilation order. I have used three ministries (worship/preaching service, Sunday school, and a small group) as an example for you. Now you have in front of you the big picture of what your church is doing (its primary ministries) and the reasons for them (characteristics of maturity).

Maturity Matrix

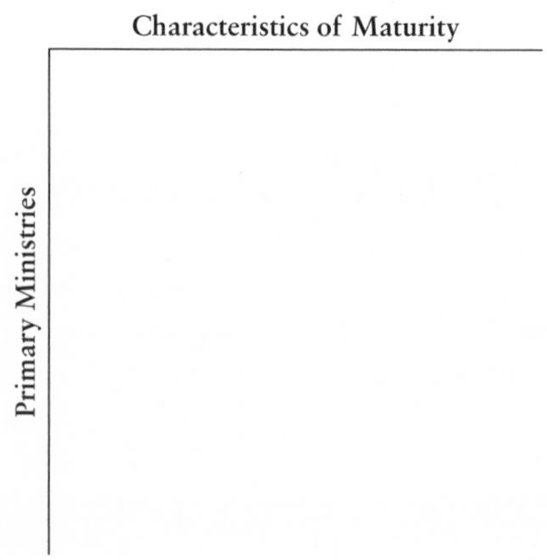

Characteristics of Maturity

Primary Ministries

Characteristics of Maturity

	Conversion (Evangelism)	Community (Fellowship)	Celebration (Worship)	Contribution (Service)	Cultivation (Teaching)
Worship/ Preaching Service					
Sunday School					
Small Group					

Step 3: Evaluation

Measure or evaluate each primary ministry for spiritual impact. To do the evaluation, the ministry team should ask the following questions of each primary ministry on the vertical axis. Note that there are boxes corresponding to each heading on the horizontal and vertical axes. As you evaluate each ministry, put a check in the box to show that a certain ministry promotes the development of a certain characteristic.

1. *Is this ministry designed to develop at least one of the characteristics of maturity in our disciples' lives?* (Some may develop more than one.) And is it doing so?

2. *How well is this ministry developing that characteristic?* The answer may be found in the numbers—people vote with their feet. How many people are attending, and is that number growing? (As I will argue in the next chapter, you must keep accurate records of attendance of your main ministries.) I encourage you to do annual quantitative research (a congregational survey or analysis) and qualitative research (one-on-one interviews with key people) of your congregation that will give you an even more accurate read than the attendance numbers do, as Willow Creek Community Church has discovered. I do understand that some pastors simply aren't wired to do this and even the thought is intimidating. However, a large church will have an executive or administrative person who may have the needed skills. A small church could recruit a layperson who is so wired and could take responsibility for such an endeavor.

3. *Do any ministries need to be tweaked or even replaced?* Every ministry has a shelf life. Some ministries simply outlive their effectiveness, and there comes a time when they need to be replaced. You must consider whether now is the time.

4. *Are there any ministries that do not develop any characteristics of maturity?* If so, do you need to change or even eliminate these ministries?

5. *Are there any characteristics of maturity that no primary ministry develops?* Inevitably, when I take churches through this fifth question, the two characteristics that are most often missed are evangelism and service. Most churches' ministries fail to develop these two essential characteristics of maturity. For those that are not doing evangelism, I sometimes suggest that they add Willow Creek Church's first two steps—build a relationship with a lost person and share a verbal witness—to their primary ministries. Another option for those who include small groups as a primary ministry is to include a service and evangelism component to what they do in their small groups. Each small group would embrace a particular ministry within or outside the church, and they all could go through evangelism training. An advantage of doing this in the small groups is that they can hold one another accountable. For those that have only a "faithful few" (usually around 20 percent or less) involved in service, I suggest adding a service component to their primary ministries. But explain to your people that they will go through the training for service only one time or once every few years.

6. *Are you aware of other churches' primary ministries?* How other churches minister may be a reflection of their unique communities. Such knowledge could be helpful to you as you tweak or even renovate your primary ministries, especially if the other churches are located in an area of the country that is similar to yours. I provided several examples earlier in this chapter. The example of Willow Creek follows.

Willow Creek

I suspect that some readers, especially those of the emergent generation and those in smaller churches, may be a little turned off by my using Willow Creek as an example, because it is a Boomer megachurch. However, they are one of the few churches in North America who are doing with profound results the kind of diagnosis that I am suggesting. In 1992 two staff persons (Greg Hawkins and Cally Parkinson) with help from an outside consultant (Eric Arnson) began to conduct congregational research, attempting to gain a unique understanding of the spiritual lives of Willow's people—how they grow and what the church could do to help them. They conducted both quantitative research that involved surveying their people and qualitative research that involved personal, one-on-one interviews. This was an extensive project that they now pursue every three years. While this is a good process, I am not convinced that you will have to do the same extensive and elaborate kind of research to discover useful information. A church can design a single survey and conduct personal interviews with core leadership, such as a board, church staff, and key lay leaders. I have included in appendix D some questions that can be used quantitatively (in a broad congregational survey) or qualitatively (in one-on-one personal interviews) in designing a tool to use with a congregation.

When Willow conducted their research, what they discovered caused them to rethink everything about how to do church. For example, they found that one-third of their congregation drove more than thirty minutes to get to church, and these people were not inviting their unchurched friends to attend the services (a key aspect of Willow's strategy), nor were these people involved in Willow's other ministries. They also discovered that their church activities alone did not drive spiritual growth and that the role of the church in people's lives changes as they mature, providing them with opportunities to serve more than with organized teaching and connecting opportunities. In short, as their people matured, they played more of a role in their own spiritual development than did the church. This included personal spiritual disciplines, such as prayer, Bible study, journaling, and so forth.

As many of you know, it is easier to talk about tweaking and changing ministries than it is to actually pull it off, especially when dealing with primary ministries. Many people find comfort in routines, even when the spiritual effectiveness has long since worn off. This is where loving strength and leadership cultivation pay rich spiritual dividends. Teach your key leaders and bring them along until they can view and embrace change as a friend. There still may be bullies who rebel or attack your leadership and attempt to persuade others to side with them so that changes are not made, and you will have to deal with them. It is imperative that this kind of behavior not be tolerated. People who bully and attack leadership must be formally disciplined, according to the procedures spelled out in your church constitution.

Factors That May Affect Primary Ministries

As you may have noted so far in this chapter, there are several factors that affect the kinds of ministries that appear on the vertical axis of the Maturity Matrix. These factors may also help you as you measure and evaluate your primary ministries. The following factors may affect a church's primary ministries and how it conducts those ministries.

Predominant Generations

The predominant generation or generations (Builders, Boomers, Bridgers) in a church will affect the primary ministries. For example, you minister differently to Builders than you do to Boomers. While the marks of a disciple's maturity are the same for each generation, the ministries that produce them in the disciple will often be different. An example is style of worship. Each generation seems to prefer a different style of worship, ranging from the great hymns of the faith for older congregants to a praise format for Boomers to a "vintage-faith" worship gathering for the younger members. And a liturgical approach will appeal to others.

The Church's Location

Another factor that affects primary ministries is the location of the church. Is it located in rural, suburban, or urban America? Location affects the church's ministry mind-set. My experience is that rural churches tend to be resistant to more contemporary ways of doing ministry. They are slow to try new approaches, preferring the tried and true. And the result is that many of these churches are not surviving. However, some urban and many suburban churches are ready to blaze new ministry trails.

The Church's Ethnicity

A third factor that affects primary ministries is the church's ethnicity. A black church may prefer to take the offering differently than a predominantly white church. Some black congregations are used to an offering walk where the congregation goes to the front of the sanctuary to drop their offering in a plate located there. And others prefer to pass a plate. And some Anglos are concerned about sending the wrong message, so they place a plate or box on a table in the back of the worship area. Traditional black churches aren't afraid to let their services go on for more than an hour, with lots of music and a lengthy sermon. However, they tend not to be as involved in small-group ministries.

The Church's Size

The size of the church will also affect the types of ministries it offers. Larger churches do ministry differently than smaller churches. For example, larger churches can offer different worship venues because they have enough people to provide multiple services, whereas some smaller churches may struggle to fill one service.

Confidence in Pastoral Leadership

A fifth factor is the church's confidence in the pastor's leadership. I have been in situations where lay leaders questioned the senior pastor's competence. Consequently, when he addressed issues affecting the core ministries in the church, these people either ignored his ideas or argued with him for their own views. Note that in these situations these pastors have lost the confidence and trust of their people and are likely on their way out.

Some pastors may have more support, but still there may be a group of people who struggle with pride, are not teachable, and feel they know more than the pastor. Incompetent or questionable pastoral leadership is an issue that a church must address if it hopes to be a Great Commission church that makes authentic disciples.

Factors Affecting Primary Ministries
Predominant Generation
Church's Location
Church's Ethnicity
Church's Size
Confidence in Pastoral Leadership

Communicating the Primary Ministries

Communication both informs and reminds people of the church's primary or core ministries—the ones that will aid them in moving toward spiritual maturity. My experience as a church consultant is that few churches communicate well, and most do not communicate enough. There are a number of practical ways to communicate your ministries to your people.

The Sermon

The most obvious means of communication is the sermon. Because of the importance of the church's core ministries, the preacher would be wise to mention them often any way he can, whether he is preaching specifically on the ministries or using them as an example or in an illustration.

New Members Class

When people join a church, especially younger people, they are sending the message that they are ready to commit to the church and its ministries. The new members class is a way to make sure they know what the ministries are. This is the time to present and explain the reason the ministries are important as well as the purpose of each. In my church we ask our new members to sign a covenant of commitment to four areas, one of which is to serve in our ministries.

You should be aware that some churches struggle with the concept of membership. When people hear the term, they are reminded of churches that stress membership for all the wrong reasons, such as a desire to be the biggest church in the denomination for "bragging" purposes. If your people struggle with the term *membership*, use a different term, such as *partners* and *partnership*, that better communicates your expectations of them.

Sunday School

The Sunday school class, ABF (Adult Bible Fellowship), or youth group can aid communication by regularly reminding people of the reasons they are in the class and its role in the church's mission, as well as in helping them become mature disciples.

Website

The younger generation is techno savvy and used to getting much of their information on the Internet. Many will check out the church on its website before ever showing up at a service. Others who are already part of the church will depend on the website to some degree to know what is going on in the church. So make sure you post information about your ministries.

Brochures

Churches that communicate well produce quality brochures that explain their values, mission, vision, and strategy. They are also an excellence source of information on the ministries that the church offers.

A Video Production

A DVD presentation of the church's ministries is an effective way to communicate important information. I had one student who produced a DVD as his class project. The video recorded ministries in action and in this way communicated that his church provided for making disciples.

A Visual

A visual object that depicts your vertical axis of ministries can be a memorable way to communicate. Andy Stanley, who pastors North Pointe Church near Atlanta, Georgia, uses the rooms of a house to explain his church's ministries. When those who attend his worship service walk into the auditorium, they see three rooms of a house up on stage. Then Stanley walks them through the rooms, explaining how the foyer corresponds to the worship service, the living room represents the Bible study events, and finally the kitchen depicts the church's small group meetings.

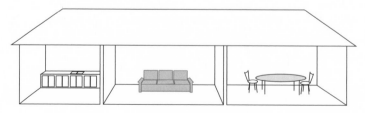

An apple, several arrows, a tree, or even a stool have been used to communicate a church's ministries. The various parts of the apple, such as the skin, flesh, and core could depict your primary ministries. Depending on the number of ministries, you could use three or four arrows that point inward toward one another. Each arrow represents a ministry, and they rotate around words such as "A passionate follower of Christ." Often Scripture uses a tree as a symbol of spiritual strength (see, for example, Jer. 17:7–8). A three- or four-legged stool, with each leg representing a ministry, is also a good illustration.

The pastor of the church could follow Stanley's example and, when preaching on the topic, include the visual illustration. For example, he could place the stool next to the pulpit and sit on it as a disciple. Then he could point to the various legs, explaining how they represent the primary ministries and how they are necessary to support the maturing disciple.

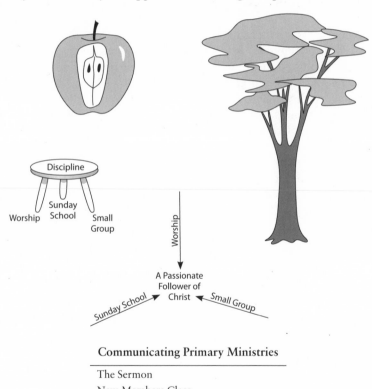

Communicating Primary Ministries

The Sermon

New Members Class

Sunday School Class/ABF/Youth Group

Website

Brochures

Video Production

Visual Illustration

Questions for Reflection and Discussion

1. Write all of your church's ministries on a piece of paper or a whiteboard. Identify your primary ministries. Those that are left are your secondary ministries.

2. Draw a Maturity Matrix, or use the one in appendix C, and write your marks or characteristics of a disciple on the horizontal axis. Then place your primary ministries on the vertical axis. Do you have any characteristics that are not supported by a ministry? If so, which ones? Do you have any ministries that do not support any of the characteristics? If so, which ones?

3. Who will construct this matrix? If a team will do it, who will they be—ministry staff, a strategic planning team, or others? Why might you opt for team involvement as opposed to having one person, such as the pastor, do it?

4. Using the Maturity Matrix, do you find that any ministries need to be tweaked or replaced? If so, which ones? When and how will you go about changing them? Will you use the matrix regularly to check on the relevance of your primary ministries?

5. If you decide you need to change or replace some of the primary ministries, what ministries will replace them? Have you looked at the ministries of other like-minded churches? If so, how might they fit into your church?

6. How many secondary ministries did you identify in question 1? Do you need to eliminate some of them? If so, which ones? How will you handle the potentially negative response of those involved in these ministries? Is there a way that some of these ministries might legitimately be combined with your primary ministries?

9

ARE YOU MAKING DISCIPLES?

Measuring Mature Disciples

At this point in the book you should have in place at least a preliminary strategy or pathway for making and then developing mature disciples in your church. This strategy is a combination of both your characteristics of maturity and your primary ministries. From this point on you will review and tweak this strategy to make sure that yours is a functioning Great Commission church. But that is not enough. You are not through yet. If the mission or mega-goal of the church is to make disciples, you must begin to ask how you are doing. Are you making disciples? It is that simple. Thus the next stage is to come up with a tool to help you regularly determine if you are making disciples and how well you are making them. This chapter will help school you to develop such a tool by presenting the evaluation problem, explaining the purposes for, and leading you through the process of evaluation.

The Problem of Evaluation

Let's face it, few people enjoy giving or receiving evaluation. It just is not much fun. I suspect this explains why so few churches have in place an intentional, formal evaluation process. Does your church have one? It seems strange for churches not to have a process of evaluation, because, as we'll see below, all churches are evaluated, whether they realize it or not.

Evaluation Is Biblical

The first-century churches were involved in evaluation.

The book of Acts. Throughout the book of Acts, Luke pauses to give us reports on how the church is progressing (Acts 1:15; 2:41, 47; 4:4; 5:14; 6:1, 7; 9:31, 35, 42; 11:21, 24; 14:1, 21; 16:5; 17:4, 12; 18:8, 10; 19:26; 21:20), and he uses numbers to do so. I understand that many people, especially those who attend small churches, are turned off by numbers. However, we must note that in Acts 2:41 and 4:4 Luke uses numbers to signal that the Jerusalem church is strong in evangelism. When we go to a doctor for a physical, he checks such vital signs as our blood pressure, pulse, and temperature and reports their status using numbers. Just as these numbers reflect our physical health, so counting heads in churches can reflect spiritual health.

Revelation 2–3. God evaluates six of his churches in Revelation 2 and 3 by pointing to their strengths and weaknesses. For example, he evaluates the church in Ephesus in Revelation 2:1–7. In verses 1–3 he points out where the church is doing well: they worked hard, did not tolerate wicked people, exposed false apostles, endured hardships, and persevered for the faith. But they had some weaknesses, according to verses 4–7: they had forsaken their first love and needed to repent of this. Also attached to this evaluation was a warning. If they did not repent, God would remove them as a church.

1 Timothy 3:1–13. Paul lists the qualifications for being an elder or overseer and a deacon in 1 Timothy 3:1–13. The elders or overseers were the first-century pastors of house churches. In verse 2 Paul writes that the overseer must be "above reproach" and goes on to list qualifications. I believe that this first statement is a summary that is fleshed out by the following qualifications. It functions as a topic sentence, and the rest of the passage provides the details or explains what it means to be above reproach. I suspect that Paul listed these qualifications for several reasons, specifically so that the overseers might know if they were qualified to pastor a house church and so the house churches would know if the overseers were qualified to lead them. Regardless of the reasons, evaluation took place, as it did with the deacons in verses 8–13.

1 Corinthians 11:28. Paul encourages the church to do self-evaluation before they partake of the Lord's Supper. His words in 1 Corinthians 11:28 teach us that partaking of the Lord's Supper is serious spiritual business. He warns in verse 27: "Therefore, whoever eats the bread or drinks the cup of the Lord in an unworthy manner will be guilty of sinning against the body and blood of the Lord." Thus, whenever we partake, we must do so in a worthy manner, which means we must pause and do a self-examination.

Some Biblical Passages on Evaluation

Acts 1:15; 2:41, 47; 4:4; 5:14; 6:1, 7; 9:31, 35, 42; 11:21, 24; 14:1, 21; 16:5; 17:4, 12; 18:8, 10; 19:26; 21:20

Revelation 2–3

1 Timothy 3:1–13

1 Corinthians 11:28

Informal Evaluation

We must realize that evaluation of our ministries and of us takes place whether we like it or not. In the majority of cases it takes place informally.

Visitors. A couple visits your church, and afterward they evaluate your ministry with answers to such questions as the following: Did you like the service? Did you like the sermon? Did you like the worship? Did you have a good experience? Did you like the preacher or the pastor? Did you like the people? Were they friendly? Do you want to go back?

Parents and children. Parents will ask their kids: Did you like the church? Did you learn anything? Would you be open to inviting friends to come and visit this church? Do you want to go back? And their child will make the decision as to whether they will return.

Women. Women have a special set of questions. They ask: Was the nursery clean? Were the bathrooms clean? Were the women friendly? Are there some women attending whom I would like to get to know? Does the church sponsor a women's Bible study? Is the church family friendly?

Men. Men tend to ask: Are there many men who attend this church? Am I one of few men present? Do I feel comfortable as a man attending this church? Did I meet any men or observe any whom I would like to get to know? Is there a men's Bible study? Is the pastor masculine? (You might question this, but just ask a man if he looks for this quality in a pastor.) If the man is a Christian, he may ask, are there any ministries for men?

Unbelievers. Finally, unbelievers ask the following: Were the people open, friendly, and inviting? Were they my kind of people? Do we have anything in common? Was it a pleasant, nonthreatening experience? Are these people for real? Did I understand what was going on? Was it for me or only for the "insiders"? Did I meet God there? Did I sense his presence? Did I learn something about God? Do I want to go back?

The point is that every church is evaluated informally. There is no escaping it. So if others are evaluating your church, shouldn't you do a formal evaluation of your church's disciple-making process, among other things, and benefit from evaluation rather than be the victim of the evaluation of others?

The Purposes of Evaluation

I would hope that by now you are convinced of the need for evaluation. If not, then the following is written for you. You might also want to use this information to convince others within your church to pursue evaluation, especially of your primary disciple-making ministries.

Prioritizes Ministry Accomplishment

It's been said that what gets evaluated gets done, and what you measure is what you get! It would be impossible to evaluate or measure everything. However, what we choose to evaluate sends a message to our people. It drives a stake in the ground that says, "This is important and something else is not as important." For example, if we evaluate our primary ministries, this signals to all involved (the senior pastor, any staff who head up those ministries, and any laypersons who are a part of them) that these are high-priority ministries from which much is expected. The result is that the people involved will focus on their part or role in making these ministries the very best they can be.

Six Purposes of Evaluation

Evaluation prioritizes ministry accomplishment.

Encourages Ministry Appraisal

A second purpose for evaluation is ministry appraisal. People who are leading and serving in the primary ministries need to know how they are doing. It is not unusual for a person to spend a year or more in ministry, thinking that all is well, only to discover, when he or she is abruptly dismissed, that it was not going well. This is unfair to the person. He or she needs an early-warning system.

Some churches respond to poor job performance in another way. They simply refuse to deal with individuals who do not have the abilities to do their job, who constantly show poor work habits, or who may be abusive. These churches feel that they are not being nice to these people, or they feel sorry for them, or they worry about what others will think if they dismiss them, or they think that it is not the Christian thing to do to dismiss people. The problem with this thinking and practice is that it makes everyone else's job more difficult. Others have to pick up the slack, or, in some cases, take unnecessary abuse. Long-term bending over backward for and coddling this kind of worker weakens, frustrates, and diminishes the entire organization.

A fair approach in every employment situation is regular ministry appraisal, when a supervisor or mentor sits down with the employee and identifies problems and deficiencies along with the person's strengths. When this is done, people know where the problems lie and what they must do to improve in their primary ministry areas, which will be reviewed again at the next appraisal. If no progress is made or can be made, the church has proper grounds for shifting the individual to another ministry within the church, for discipline, or for dismissal. Sometimes, when church leaders lack the courage to dismiss an individual whose performance is not acceptable, they shift him or her to another position. Again, this is detrimental to the entire ministry.

Some people believe that it is not Christian to fire or dismiss a person, but in reality it is not Christian to keep the person on staff. People who are not functioning well in a ministry are usually aware of it and need to find a ministry where they fit and function well. Because they may be afraid to venture out on their own, they cling to the current position—to everyone's detriment, theirs and the others in the ministry. Sometimes it takes a dismissal to prod a person to find where he or she really fits.

Six Purposes of Evaluation

Evaluation prioritizes ministry accomplishment.
Evaluation encourages ministry appraisal.

Fosters Ministry Affirmation

I consider that affirming people who are serving in our disciple-making ministries is one of the most important purposes for evaluation. In my experience as a consultant, pastor of three churches, and interim preacher in numerous churches across several different denominations, I have learned that the people who make up the average church tend not to affirm those who are serving them well, whether on a pastoral or lay level. They appreciate competence in ministry, especially the primary ones, but are slow to affirm those who achieve it. They seem more willing to be critical than complimentary. I believe that they assume the individuals who serve well are aware of their accomplishments and the impact they are having, but this is usually not the case. Proverbs 16:24 says, "Pleasant words are a honeycomb, sweet to the soul and healing to the bones." Who does not look forward to the day when the Savior will say, "Well done, good and faithful servant"?

I recall how in one church where I was consulting, a lady who led the children's ministry looked at me and the others assembled and said, "It sure would be nice if on occasion someone said 'thank you' and showed a little gratitude for what we do. But that just does not happen around here."

How can we regularly affirm those in our churches who minister well? How can we make sure that acknowledging a good job does not fall through the cracks—that it happens around here? The answer is regular evaluation. Most turn up their nose at evaluation because it frightens and even intimidates them, but identifying problems is only one side of evaluation. The other side is affirmation. If we evaluate workers several times a year, then even when no one else affirms them, they will receive needed, valued affirmation. I will say more about the frequency of evaluation below.

Six Purposes of Evaluation

Evaluation prioritizes ministry accomplishment.
Evaluation encourages ministry appraisal.
Evaluation fosters ministry affirmation.

Supports Ministry Correction

Affirmation is one very important side of the appraisal coin; correction is the other. The word sounds ominous and conjures up images of difficult times, discipline, and chastisement. Some hear the word *correction* and envision a harsh father with a strap in his hand. While correction frightens most of us, it is a much needed but most often neglected aspect of leadership and pastoral ministry. No one wants to do the correcting or chastising or be on the receiving end, but in a fallen world it has become a necessary fact of life. Scripture teaches that God disciplines us for our good (Heb. 12:10). Should churches not follow suit?

When assessment takes place, we discover that all of us have areas that need correction. We have blind spots. There are things we may not perceive as problems, which hamper our primary ministry efforts. These could include a distracting mannerism, an irritating tone of voice, a gesture that detracts from a pastor's message, an annoying sense of humor, or inappropriate clothing for the job. Most people can correct these after they are made aware of them, but it will not happen unless some kind of appraisal system is in place to call attention to the problem.

Correction is also needed when the sinful nature, as Paul calls it in Galatians 5:16–21, is allowed to dominate. The acts of the sinful nature indicate that one is not being led by the Spirit (vv. 17–18). This happens far too often in ministry. How do leaders know when the sinful nature predominates in their lives? Hopefully someone will confront them. This is not likely to happen unless a regular performance-appraisal system provides the opportunity to surface and deal with the problem.

So an important aspect of correction is staff evaluation. When a staff person is not performing up to reasonable expectations, a superior needs to address the problem, stating exactly what the problem is and what must be done to correct it, and making himself or herself available to help the person. Reevaluation should be done after a month or two. If the staff person shows no improvement, additional steps should be taken to correct the situation. If it still does not change, the staff person may need to be fired. However, the advantage of evaluation with correction is that the individual will likely resign before it gets to a dismissal. This is good for two reasons. First, people in the church who might find fault are not able to do so because the person resigned. Second, it is less likely a staff person would attempt to sue you or the ministry if he or she has resigned.

Six Purposes of Evaluation

Evaluation prioritizes ministry accomplishment.
Evaluation encourages ministry appraisal.
Evaluation fosters ministry affirmation.
Evaluation supports ministry correction.

Leads to Ministry Improvement

Inviting and accepting critique is difficult, but the result can and must be learning that leads to improvement in all areas of ministry—secondary as well as primary. Obtaining objective feedback from someone who is more experienced and qualified in our area of ministry is invaluable for those who desire to be the best at what they do for the Savior.

As hard as it is to hear, we desperately need people in our life who will bravely and honestly tell us when something is not working. This is how we get better at what we do. If we choose to enclose ourselves in a comfortable, nonconfrontational ministry cocoon, we will likely create ministry that is much less than it could be for Christ. We need people—hopefully but not necessarily loving people—who provide an objective, informed perspective of what we are attempting for our Lord.

I cannot emphasize enough the importance of good ministry appraisal in assessing our primary ministries and those who lead them. The benefits far outweigh the disadvantages. Greg Hawkins, the executive pastor at Willow Creek Community Church, writes of their congregational evaluation: "It has caused us to rethink *everything* about how we do church."[1] And senior pastor Bill Hybels adds, "Facts are your friends—challenging friends, yet friends nonetheless."[2]

There are some liabilities involved in evaluation, and you must watch for these. First, evaluation has the potential to terrify volunteers, especially those in up-front positions. The thought that someone is critiquing them is often unnerving. So initially, cut them some slack, and make sure they understand why you do evaluation. Also, in situations where you ask someone to evaluate you, you are giving that person a certain amount of authority over you. Be careful whom you choose. We have found that too much evaluation can create an environment of constant criticism in the church. Ask yourself and others, have we become more critical in a negative sense than we were before we started the evaluation process? Finally, an overemphasis on assessment can destroy enthusiasm, creativity, and spontaneity in the ministry. But using evaluation as a time for affirmation can be a wonderful corrective and possible preventative of any of these outcomes.

Six Purposes of Evaluation

Evaluation prioritizes ministry accomplishment.

Evaluation encourages ministry appraisal.

Evaluation fosters ministry affirmation.

Evaluation supports ministry correction.

Evaluation leads to ministry improvement.

Promotes Ministry Change

Evaluation promotes ministry change. There, I said it—the C word. But I do not apologize for using it. I argue that a church that does not change is out of the will of God. This is because Christianity from start to finish is all about change or spiritual transformation, which is the biblical term for change (Rom. 12:2; 2 Cor. 3:18).

To get better at what we do as well as grow spiritually, we must always be improving the way we do things. In some churches this requires deep change because they have changed very little in the last twenty to thirty years. Now if they are to survive, they must undergo extensive change. Some in the corporate world argue that often this is the best way to help a business turn around. But, of course, the church is a different entity. It is a voluntary organization where people "vote with their feet." Change, at least massive change, in smaller, older churches is such a daunting process that it is not likely to happen. When a church has resisted change for a long time and then tries to institute change, it seldom survives. It's too much for the church to handle. Sometimes it is better to let a church die and release its people to attend other, healthier churches. This is painful, rather like burying an older family member.

There are other churches that appear on the surface to be very innovative and change-oriented, but they need to change too. A great example is Willow Creek Community Church. Greg Hawkins explains, "Honestly, it took a while for all of this to sink in. We went through our own stages of denial—anger, sadness, depression, the works—until we could finally embrace the brutal truth: we needed to change."[3]

The key is incremental change, or what I refer to as "tweak change." We accomplish "tweak change" through regular, timely evaluation—we "tweak" our primary ministries here and there. At its most basic level, each week we ask, How can I do it better next time or how can we better make disciples? After a year or more, you will discover that you are not the same church. You are a spiritually stronger church, but though the changes may be extensive, they have been gradual and few may have even noticed.

Six Purposes of Evaluation

Evaluation prioritizes ministry accomplishment.

Evaluation encourages ministry appraisal.

Evaluation fosters ministry affirmation.

Evaluation supports ministry correction.

Evaluation leads to ministry improvement.

Evaluation promotes ministry change.

Doing Evaluation

Now that you understand the problems and purposes of evaluation, we need to look at the process of evaluating discipleship in the church. It is a four-step process. First, you need to decide who will lead the process. Second, you will need to determine whom you will evaluate. Third, you must determine what you will evaluate, and finally, how often you will evaluate.

Step 1: Determine Who Will Lead

Someone must lead the evaluation process. Without leadership it will not happen, and the pastor may or may not choose to lead it. In a larger church an executive or administrative pastor may take the lead. This was the case at Willow Creek Community Church. Pastor Greg Hawkins led the way, assisted by Cally Parkinson, Willow's communications director. In a smaller church it could be a layperson who would lead the evaluation process. If it's not possible to evaluate all the ministries of the church, at least the disciple-making ministries must be evaluated. This is so important that it works best when the senior pastor leads the process. Not only does he need to know what is going on, but his involvement sends a message to everyone of the importance of measurement.

Step 2: Determine Who Will Be Evaluated

The key people involved in the disciple-making process must be evaluated. This would include the senior pastor and any ministry staff who head up the primary ministries in your church. In a smaller church context, it could be the pastor and any layperson who heads up a ministry. If there is a governing board, the members of the board should be evaluated to determine if they support the disciple-making process and if they are committed to and involved in the process.

The purpose of evaluation is to determine the effectiveness of ministry. My experience in churches is that when you have the right people in the right places, they produce, which is reflected most often in attendance. Again, people "vote with their feet." I do realize that in saying this, I alienate some staff people. This gets us into the quality versus quantity debate. Some argue that numbers or quantity is not always an indication of quality ministry. I have found this to be true only in rare occasions. Quality and quantity walk hand in hand. If I found that a staff person was not producing, I would attempt to find out why. Is this person wired to do what he or she is doing? Does the person need more training? Does the person agree with our mission, vision, core values, and strategy for making disciples? The evaluation process can answer these questions. If there is a problem, the number of times the person is evaluated should be increased. Should the situation not get better, then often the staff person or leader will resign, which is best for all involved and avoids potentially messy legal problems.

Step 3: Determine What to Evaluate

Before discussing what you will evaluate, I need to say something about record keeping. It is important to keep good records of what is taking place in the disciple-making process. This means keeping good statistics, so do not be afraid of or resistant to numbers. Remember Bill Hybels's statement: "Facts are your friends!" I state the obvious because often the kinds of "hard charging" pastors who lead churches well are averse to statistics. And this was true of Hybels.

You do not have to have a lot of information, just the right information. The primary statistics you need to keep and follow are attendance figures—the number of people attending your primary ministries for making disciples. Other information you may want to keep track of is the number of people who accept Christ, as reflected by baptisms, and the percentage of people who get involved in small groups or some form of service or church ministry. This information should be available to the governing board and any staff.

Now we turn to what you will evaluate. You must not attempt to evaluate everything. That would be evaluation overkill. Instead, evaluate that which is most important to the ministry. I recommend the following three areas: clarity of the process, number of committed people, and attainment of goals.

CLARITY OF THE PROCESS

You will want to assess the clarity of your disciple-making process. Do people understand the process? Are they getting it? I have noted that the majority of the churches with whom I consult—some of the leading churches for their size in America—struggle with communication. One way to determine if people understand the process is to ask them. Another is to track the numerical growth of the ministries.

NUMBER OF COMMITTED PEOPLE

You will want to determine how many people are in the process or have committed to it. The way to measure this is to count heads. If Luke did it, there is no reason why we should not (see Acts 2:41; 4:4). Note weekly how many people attend your worship services and your other primary disciple-making ministries—small groups, Sunday school. You could do the same for your secondary ministries to keep track of how they are doing as well. Remember, poor performance of the secondary ministries is cause for discontinuing them.

Assessment will show if the numbers are increasing from week to week. Note if attendance is increasing in some ministries but decreasing in others. For example, is the worship service growing numerically but the small groups are staying the same or even declining? This would indicate a problem with those that are decreasing.

Having stressed the importance of numbers, I must add that numbers are not the only measure that you look at. While Luke stressed the importance of numbers in Acts, I noted at the beginning of the chapter some other forms of measurement or evaluation. For example, Paul had a list of the qualifications for elders (pastors) and deacons in 1 Timothy 3:1–13 (he had a similar list in Titus 1:6–9). My view is that these were not only for the use of the congregation in evaluating the qualifications of elders and deacons but for the elders and deacons to evaluate themselves. Also Paul encouraged the congregation as individuals to evaluate themselves before they partook of communion (1 Cor. 11:28). Thus, an aspect of measuring the church's core disciple-making ministries is annually to ask its disciples both one-on-one (qualitative evaluation) and as a congregation (quantitative evaluation) to evaluate them and how they impact the people. Are they working or not? The former can use such means as focus groups and one-on-one interviews. The latter could be done through congregational surveys online or sent to homes by mail.

I can see the look of horror on some of your faces! You are thinking, *I could never do that! I am simply not wired that way. I could never do any kind of evaluation.* This is what Bill Hybels and many of the leaders at Willow Creek thought, yet under the direction of Greg Hawkins, who *is* wired that way, measurement has become a key focus that affects the direction of the church, according to Hawkins and Parkinson's book *Reveal: Where Are You?*

ATTAINMENT OF GOALS

You will want to evaluate how well you are accomplishing any goals you may have set for the primary disciple-making ministries. If you set ministry goals, it is imperative that you assess how well you are accomplishing them. Here are six goals or "church health indicators" used and regularly assessed by Saddleback Community Church.

We'd like to see 80 percent of our members in some type of small group.

We want 100 percent of our new believers personally contacted and encouraged.

We want one leader for every 10 people.

We want at least 50 percent of our members involved in ministry.

We want to start at least one new mission a year.

We want more than 50 percent of our new members to be through baptism [not just coming from another church].[4]

Step 4: Determine How Often to Evaluate

The disciple-making process is so important to the life of your church and fulfilling the Great Commission that you will want to keep constant tabs on how you are doing. If I were a pastor, I would want the attendance figures for the primary ministries on my desk each Monday morning, but a down week should not be cause for alarm. You can better tell how you are doing by looking at monthly and quarterly attendance figures that are averages of weekly and monthly attendance. Assessing the monthly and quarterly figures provides a better read and will reveal trends. A weekly evaluation can be helpful in discovering bad versus good attendance weekends and whether they are the same year after year. If the latter is the case, then you could plan in advance to offset poor attendance weekends, perhaps by inviting a special guest speaker or addressing a topic that many would want to hear.

As a consultant, when I view a church's attendance figures, I find few surprises. I know that the summer months of June and July are hard on church attendance. Most people choose to go on vacation during these months. I used to include August, but some public schools have begun to start up in August so that most people vacation earlier in the summer. Perhaps the worst period for church attendance is mid to late July. Other weekends are July 4, Super Bowl weekend, Memorial Day, Thanksgiving, and Labor Day. So take these times into consideration in your planning and evaluation of your core ministries.

The Evaluation Process

Step 1: Determine who will lead the process.

Step 2: Determine who will be evaluated.

Step 3: Determine what to evaluate.

Step 4: Determine how often to evaluate.

Questions for Reflection and Discussion

1. Why do you think so few churches and ministry organizations do evaluation? Does your ministry have an intentional, formal process in place? Why or why not? If not, what do you plan to do about it?

2. What impact does the fact that evaluation took place in the first-century church have on you? Does it help persuade you to put a plan for evaluation in place? Why or why not? Would this information help you to persuade the board, staff, or church that you need to do evaluation, especially of your primary, core ministries?

3. Do the informal evaluation questions sound familiar to you? Do you find yourself asking these same questions about your ministries? Why or why not?

4. The author argues that because informal evaluation takes place, the church should implement a formal evaluation program and benefit from it. Does this make sense?

5. Who can take charge of evaluating the disciple-making process in your church? Why?

6. Who will be evaluated? Why?

7. How will the programs be evaluated? Why?

8. How often will the programs be evaluated—weekly, monthly, quarterly, all of the above?

9. What weekends have proved historically to be low attendance weekends in your community?

10

HOW TO RECRUIT THE RIGHT STAFF

Staffing for the Development of Mature Disciples

After reading chapter 9, you might assume that the only use for the Maturity Matrix is to design, evaluate, and explain or communicate your disciple-making process to all involved in the ministry. But there is more to it than that. You now have a basic, working disciple-making plan in place that might not be the finished product but is moving in that direction. However, without the right personnel and proper funding, even the best strategy will not achieve the intended goals. Thus I encourage you to read on, because this chapter on staffing and the next one on budgeting have important information for the disciple-making process.

Staffing for Maturity

Who will be involved in reaching your community and making them disciples? Who makes up the ministry team? Who will help implement your disciple-making process? As you answer these questions, remember that your church is only as good as the people who make up the team. Peter Drucker is right when he writes, "People determine the performance capacity of an organization. No organization can do better than the people it has."[1] The personnel principle is that it takes good people to lead and build good disciple-making ministries. You can develop an excellent disciple-making process, but it will not mean much if you do not have the right people to deliver it.

These people make up your ministry team. Though I am not aware of any passage that commands believers to work in teams, team ministry is modeled effectively throughout the Old and New Testaments. In Exodus 18 Jethro (Moses's father-in-law) rescued him from ministry burnout by directing him to form a team to minister to his congregation of Israelites. In the Gospels Jesus ministered effectively through a somewhat ragtag team of disciples (Mark 3:13–19; 6:7) that became a powerful force for Jesus Christ, as we see in Acts and the Epistles. And throughout his ministry Paul was rarely seen without a team that included such people as Barnabas (Acts 11:25–26; 13:2–3), John Mark (13:5), Silas (15:40), Timothy (16:1–3), and many others. And Paul's body metaphor in 1 Corinthians 12:12–31 illustrates well the importance of a team to effective disciple making.

The reason is not complex—all of us can do more than one of us. There are some aspects of ministry that you can do better than I, and there are some that I can do better than you. Thus we are most effective for the Savior when we do them together. Leaders work ever so closely with a God-given team. And there are only a few exceptions, such as in a time of ministry crisis, when there is no time to even gather the team, or when the team cannot come to a consensus decision. In these situations, point leaders step out and lead.

When you develop a ministry team strategically, you need to examine all your people from the perspective of your disciple-making mission in general and your vision of what that looks like in particular. The vision is your God-given dream or snapshot of what all of you can accomplish for God by working in harmony together. It supplies not only a picture of where your ministry ship is sailing but a dream of who will sail with you—your disciple-making dream team.

You must select people, not on the basis of who happens to be available or already on the ministry team, but who *should be* on the team, those whom God has brought together for such a time as this. Though painful, it could mean releasing people who do not fit the team well. Your church does not exist to provide jobs for people, but to provide Christ-honoring ministry through people with the right divine wiring in the right positions. Somebody is not better than nobody when that somebody isn't right for the position. The stakes are too high for this kind of thinking that seems to permeate so many of our churches at the beginning of the twenty-first century. While no one is perfect for any position, put simply, the challenge is not finding people, it is finding the *right* people—the people God wants on your team.

The team is made up of three groups whose ministry is critical to the impact of the church on a lost, dying community. They are a godly, wise governing board (in churches that have one); a gifted, passionate, spiritually motivated staff; and a well-mobilized congregation. Working in harmony under the Holy

Spirit, all three groups have the potential to turn many in their unbelieving, unchurched community into a band of mature disciples who will serve and glorify the Savior. While all three make up your ministry dream team, in this chapter I will focus on and explore only the staff's role in making disciples. (You can read about the roles of the other two groups in chapter 10 of my book *Advanced Strategic Planning*).

In this chapter, the staff I'm referring to are the full- and part-time professional people involved in the church's ministry. A growing number may have seminary or Bible college training, and most are remunerated in some way. But we are not discussing just any staff or mix of ministry people, but rather those whom you dream about when you see yourself meaningfully involved up to your eyebrows in making disciples.

You might assume that the following is written more for churches with multiple staff; however, this is not the case. Those who lead small, growing churches will find it most instructive for putting in place a ministry dream team as increasingly they make new disciples.

The Definition of a Staff Team

A disciple-making staff team consists of two or more gifted, competent, spiritual leaders who are deeply committed to serving together to equip the congregation and develop leaders to accomplish the church's disciple-making strategy.

Two or More People

First, a dream team is made up of two or more people. It could range in number from a single, part-time bivocational pastor with a part-time volunteer secretary to more than a hundred men and women with plenty of secretarial and custodial backup in a megachurch.

Leaders

Second, these people are leaders. That means they influence people. More importantly, they are gifted, competent, and spiritually motivated leaders. While all Christians are gifted, these leaders bring to the team the right combination of gifts that complement those of any other team person. They are competent in that God has so gifted them that they are good at what they do—working in the primary or core ministries. They are also spiritually motivated. They are leaders who want to be part of the team for the right reasons. They believe that the ministry is not all about them or what it can do for them; it is about the Savior and his imperative to go and make disciples.

Committed to Serving Together

Members of the dream team are deeply committed to serving together. They are not on the team simply to collect a check. Their goal is more than just showing up each day. They have made the deepest of commitments to the team in general and its disciple-making ministry in particular. They are not the kind of people who at the slightest sign of trouble will throw up their hands and walk away. They are not working with you while waiting for a better offer. They are there for the long haul. In addition, they see themselves as Christ sees them, as his servants. They are servant leaders (Matt. 20:24–28).

Finally, they are committed to serving together. I believe that this is the most difficult part of working on a team—the working relationship. You have to get along with each other, and the team is committed to this no matter how difficult ministry may be at stressful times during the life of the church. This also means that they will work hard at dismantling any ministry silos. Any staff person who believes that his or her ministry is the most important ministry in the church and sees the other primary disciple-making ministries as less important has created a ministry silo. The result of such an attitude is that he or she diminishes the others and their ministries and fails to communicate and work together with the other staff. Ministry silos are ministry killers when it comes to making disciples and must not be tolerated in Christ's church or they will bring it to its knees.

Committed to Making Disciples

Members of the dream team are deeply committed to accomplishing the church's disciple-making strategy. The vision of the pastor or team leader has grabbed hold of them and will not let go. This is because it is God's vision as well as his mission for his church. The staff hold the same vision in common—the senior leader's dream of a disciple-making ministry is their dream as well. This vision is clearly defined and compelling, so they all see the same picture and feel the same excitement.

Recruiting Your Dream Team

How do you build a team such as this? Much of building a disciple-making team has to do with recruiting the best available people. Since the best leaders are quickly snatched up and not always available, you will need to maintain a recruitment mentality, constantly looking for good people. Recruiting a team of disciple makers involves answering a number of important recruitment questions.

When to Recruit

Only church planters have the luxury of recruiting a whole new team at once, but this can have its cons as well as pros. Chances are good that most of you reading this book have some sort of team in place already. It may be large or small, and it may or may not be a team that makes disciples. Regardless of the size, your job from now on is to build your team one person at a time. There are several indications that it is time to recruit a new team person.

Too Much Work

When things that are critical to the life of the church are not being done, not because staff members do not want to accomplish them or are letting down on the job but because they are too busy with critical ministry matters, it is time to recruit a new member of your team. When the team members are already working long hours and simply cannot get everything done, there is a need to think about adding another person to the staff.

The Church Plateaus

Another time to recruit a new staff member is when the church plateaus. One major reason the church may plateau is because it does not have enough staff or the right staff to take it to the next level. As churches grow, there is a need for new and different leadership skills and abilities on the part of the staff. Not everyone, including the senior pastor, will be able to grow with the church. Some staff prefer small churches, whereas other staff prefer growing churches. This needs to be taken into account in working out the staff equation for making disciples.

How can you know if you have enough staff? In *Staff Your Church for Growth*, Gary McIntosh provides us with the following staff ratios that should prove helpful to your situation in answering this question.[2]

Average Worship Attendance	Full-Time Staff	Support Staff
150	1	1
300	2	1.5
450	3	2
600	4	2.5
750	5	3

Should you be in a larger church, you would need to adjust these ratios to your size. Note that the average worship attendance increment is 150 people, the full-time staff is one for every 150 people, and the support staff is approximately .5 to 1 for every 150 people. Thus, if your church has 900 people, you would need 6 full-time staff and 3 to 3.5 support staff.

The best answer to the question as to when you need to recruit someone
to be part of a disciple-making team is *before* you have the need. The idea is
to bring on board the necessary full-time and support staff before you reach
a plateau or things start falling through the cracks. I know that this sounds
risky, and many would object. However, it is how you as a staff in general and
a point leader in particular proactively in faith lead the church forward. What
you must realize is that the right staff person will more than pay for him- or
herself in just a short time. The idea is to "play offense"—to use the information in the chart above to note the next increment and recruit the necessary
staff people to help lead you to it. The other option is to "play defense"—to
wait and hope that you will get to the next level, and then, when you run
into problems, hire the necessary staff. The latter is playing catch-up, and the
problem is that you may plateau before you reach the next level, and once you
plateau, it is difficult to regain ministry momentum.

Whom to Recruit

Now that you know you have a staff need, you also need to know what to
look for in a disciple-making team person.

First, you need to recruit a balanced staff team. Before I address staffing
balance, I need to identify the two kinds of staff persons. I divide them into
ministry and operational or administrative staff. The latter are made up primarily of such people as a church administrator and/or an executive pastor.
The primary ministry staff are those who take the lead in making disciples.
Some focus mainly on a particular age group, such as preschool kids, children,
youth, and adults. Because they focus so much of their time and ministry on a
specific age group, they have limited involvement with the rest of the church.
The other primary ministry staff are what I refer to as functional staff. They
focus on one of the church's functions, such as worship, evangelism, community,
service, or biblical instruction. Unlike the age-specific staff, they affect and
minister to the entire church, as the whole church is to be involved in worship,
evangelism, and the other functions.

A small, growing church or a church plant will recruit as they grow. A larger
church with several staff already on board will need to evaluate their situation
and recruit new staff as they grow and current personnel leave.

To balance a staff team, list all the age-specific staff and functional staff
that the church needs. For example, will there be a need for a preschool
staff person or someone to lead in evangelism? Then prioritize staff in both
groups. Which age-specific staff will be needed and in what order? Who is
needed first, second, and so on? Do the same with the functional staff. To

recruit a balanced primary staff team, you will need to move back and forth between the two kinds of staff as you add future personnel. For example, a new church or a small church might want to hire a worship person first. Then the next hire might be a person to work with youth. That way a church does not have a staff consisting mostly of age-specific people who minister only to a certain age group, and the same for the functional staff. What about an executive pastor? My research says that most churches secure the services of an executive pastor when their attendance reaches around seven hundred people.

In addition to the above, you are looking for balanced leaders who together, because of their commitment to making disciples, can grow the church. Making disciples means that people grow spiritually as well as in number. Spiritually healthy, biblically functioning churches grow. In time unhealthy churches plateau and begin to die. What this means is that you need to have in place a team that is balanced, accomplishing both outreach and in-reach, because making and maturing disciples involves both.

Most churches begin their lives with a strong outreach component. They are passionate about making disciples (evangelism) and then growing them into mature disciples. Often, as the church grows, leaders turn their attention to internal matters that demand their time, such as facilities and finances, and before long they may become totally focused inward.

Balancing Staff Positions

Outreach	In-Reach
Evangelism	Christian Education
Authentic Worship	Biblical Instruction
Assimilation	Administration
Missions	Teaching

COMPLEMENTARY STAFF LEADERS

A church needs to recruit leaders who complement the designs and ministries of others on the team. The pastor may be an extroverted leader with gifts of leading, teaching, and evangelism. Someone who has in-reach oriented gifts, such as administration and organization, would complement the gifts of the pastor. Though ministry is often accomplished by extroverted temperaments, some introverted temperaments are needed as well.

What to Look For

What are the criteria that a leader must meet to make your disciple-making team? The answer is the three Cs of recruitment: character, competence, and chemistry.

CHARACTER

The first criterion is character. It is the sum total of a person's qualities that reflect who a person is and what he or she does. They may be good or bad, and a recruiter should be interested in both. I have heard fellow faculty member Howard Hendricks say on a number of occasions that the greatest crisis in the world today is a crisis of leadership, and the crisis of leadership is a crisis of character. Character is critical to good leadership; thus recruitment begins with assessing personal character.

Scripture provides us with several first-century character checklists for a leader that are just as relevant and binding in the twenty-first century. Lists for men that we briefly visited in the chapter on evaluation are found in 1 Timothy 3:1–7 and Titus 1:6–9. Some character qualifications for women are found in 1 Timothy 2:9–10; 3:11; Titus 2:3–5; and 1 Peter 3:1–6. In appendix E there are a Men's Character Assessment for Ministry and a Women's Character Assessment for Ministry for your use with your team.

In terms of character qualities that can prove detrimental to a team ministry in particular, be on the lookout for people with big egos manifested by pride. Also watch for loners, people who prefer and value working alone. Finally, watch out for people who are independently successful. They have achieved their current position by doing it their way by themselves.

COMPETENCE

A second critical criterion is ministry competence. It has to do with how well people do what they do, which in this case is some aspect of making disciples. Ministry competence consists of God-given capabilities as well as developed capabilities. God-given capabilities are natural and spiritual gifts, passion, and temperament. The recruiter must ask, What are the gifts, passion, and temperament of the person whom I am looking for to fill the particular disciple-making core ministry position? Most importantly, once the primary disciple-making ministries are determined, it must be determined what the competency requirements are for the leader of each ministry. Some examples should help.

Let's begin with the senior pastor. My experience in the North American culture is that highly competent senior pastors who are doing a good job at making disciples have at least three gifts: leadership, evangelism, and communication (preaching and teaching). They are passionate about the Great Commission, and they balance accomplishing goals with being relational.

A second critical staff person for the core disciple-making ministries is the one who leads worship. This person needs a leadership gift; some kind of natural musical gifting, such as a good voice; a knowledge of and passion for worship; and possibly a temperament that focuses on the details. The worship leader does not need to be a performer as much as a person with a leadership gift who can lead the worship team and the congregation in worship.

When choosing leaders of the small groups and/or Sunday school ministries, if they are primary ministries, the needed competencies must be considered, as well. Those who lead the primary ministries may be professional people or laypersons, depending on the size of the church, but they should have the gifts and temperament needed to fulfill the position.

The *level* of competence must also be considered. The question here is how far can this person lead a ministry? One of the determining factors is the size of the church. Is he or she a small-church person, a middle-size-church person, or a large-church person? And which do you need? For example, if you are in a large church or envision leading a large church, is the person capable of ministering effectively at that level or the next level, whatever that may be? My pastor (Steve Stroope of Lake Pointe Church in Rockwall, Texas) has led our church from around forty people to six thousand. This means that he is capable of making the necessary adjustments that it takes to lead a church through its various sizes. Not everyone can do that. I believe that the more leaders understand themselves in general and their wiring or design in particular, the more they will have a feel for their level of competence. So I would explore with them their divine design. I have had men in ministry tell me that they are large-church pastors and others that they are small-church pastors. While this is an intuitive read on their part, it is probably based on their divine design or wiring. One way to know your competence level for sure is experience. If you are a church planter, you will at some point hit your level of competence as the church grows. How will you know? The church will usually stop growing and plateau.

Other characteristics of those who have a high competence ceiling and are able to lead their ministries to the next level are the following: being change-oriented, flexible, learners, comfortable with uncertainty, risk takers, task-oriented, emotionally intelligent or mature, and strategic thinkers.

Developed capabilities include character, knowledge, skills, and emotions. As I said above, character is who a person is and what he or she does. This needs to be considered in one who will lead a ministry. This person must also have certain knowledge, skills, and emotional maturity. A senior pastor must be above reproach (1 Tim. 3:2). He needs to know a number of things, such as the Bible and theology, how to lead, how to think and act strategically, a biblical theology of discipleship, and how to develop a strategy to make disciples. In regard to skills, he needs to be able to preach, lead, counsel, and so on. Finally, a senior pastor needs to be emotionally mature. I have observed a number of ministries that have fallen apart due to emotional issues affecting the team, such as anger or jealousy on the part of the senior pastor. And who has not experienced an emotionally insecure leader in ministry or the marketplace who led through fear? This is a "team breaker." As you examine potential team candidates and design potential staff positions, carefully think and work your way through these capabilities with input from your current leaders.

CHEMISTRY

A third criterion for a leader is fitting into the ministry chemistry. This is evident in several areas. First is ministry alignment. Does a potential team person have the same core values, mission, and vision as the church? And, most importantly, does he or she resonate with the church's strategy for making disciples?

Another area is theology or doctrine. Does the potential team person agree with the essentials and nonessentials of the faith? The essentials are the basic tenets of orthodox Christianity. The nonessentials are areas where there is more room for divergence, such as forms of church government, mode of baptism, and the role of women. Disagreement with the essentials would disqualify a potential team member. And any disagreement over the nonessentials should also be carefully considered, as a group's nonessentials can still be important to many in the group, especially in certain situations.

Emotional alignment is also part of the chemistry. Will the potential team member get along with the rest of the staff in general and the senior pastor in particular? This is critical because, if a disciple-making team cannot work together, they will not make disciples. Emotional alignment involves temperament, passion, and the emotional climate that the leader sets for the team.

How to Recruit

How do you recruit the disciple-making team person? Do you begin with the people whom you already have on board and design the strategy around them, or do you begin with your strategy and look for leaders who fit best? The answer is both.

THE OPTIONS

On the one hand, you can have a great team of people with a poor or nonexistent strategy, and they will accomplish much in spite of the situation. That is the nature of a good team—that is what they do. On the other hand, you can have a poor staff with a great strategy for making disciples. Without the right people on board, even the best strategy is not likely to produce results. So the key in either case is to enlist the right people for your ministry team. The ideal is to have the right people involved in the right strategy. As a senior pastor and a staff, this will be your lifetime team pursuit, combining the right people with the best strategy, and you are responsible for crafting both.

Staff versus Strategy

Strong Staff	Weak Staff
Good strategy: Growing church	Good strategy: Plateaued church
Poor strategy: Limited growth	Poor strategy: Declining church

THE FOUR Rs

Building the right disciple-making team with the right strategy involves the four Rs (see the chart below). First, in light of your strategy, you will be able to *reaffirm* some or hopefully many of your current people. They are the right people in the right place at the right time, so keep them happy. Second, you will need to *redeploy* some of your people. They are the right people who are in the wrong place at the right time. So find where in your ministry they fit best! Third, you will need to *replace* some of your current people. They are the wrong people in the wrong place at the wrong time. Do them and yourself a favor by letting them go and helping them find the right place to use their ministry skills. Some pastors attempt to redeploy people who should be replaced, which is a big mistake. It never works and only exacerbates the problem. When trying to decide whether to redeploy or replace, consider the person's character, competence, and chemistry. Poor character and chemistry are disqualifiers. However, if the person's character and chemistry are good, and he or she would be truly competent in another position on staff, then redeploy the person.

Finally, you will need to *recruit* some people. These are the right people who need to be in the right place—on your ministry team—at the right time, which is now. This is the responsibility of most senior pastors and executive pastors.

Building the Right Disciple-Making Team with the Right Strategy

Four Rs	People	Place	Time
Reaffirm	Right people	Right place	Right time
Redeploy	Right people	Wrong place	Right time
Replace	Wrong people	Wrong place	Wrong time
Recruit	Right people	Right place	Right time

Where to Recruit

The oft-debated question is, Should you recruit potential disciple-making staff from outside or inside your church? I think that the best answer is both, depending on your staff needs and circumstances.

RECRUITING FROM OUTSIDE THE CHURCH

The advantage of recruiting people from outside the church is that they bring creativity and innovation to your church, especially if they have been in a good disciple-making context, whether church or parachurch. They may think differently and have other ministry exposure than the rest of the staff, and this could refresh and invigorate your team. The downside is that you do not have as good a read on their character, their competence, their chemistry, how well they will work with you, and their commitment to what you are attempting to do. Add to this the fact that far too often other churches will give people good references when they should know better. When they do so they may have the best intentions, but they really sell the body of Christ short.

RECRUITING FROM WITHIN THE CHURCH

The advantage of recruiting leaders from within the church is the opposite of the above. Most are currently laypeople, and you should have a good read on their character, competence, chemistry, and commitment to and passion for your disciple-making strategy. The disadvantage is that they may not have the creativity and innovation that come from experiences in other ministries—unless they are creative, innovative people to begin with. To recruit a lay leader to your staff, you must have a leadership development process in place for training.

AN OPINION

Though you will likely employ both methods to form your team, a growing number of leaders are opting for the latter. For example, Bill Hybels writes, "Occasionally I'm asked where I find such great people to hire. My answer might be surprising. Almost 75 percent of our leaders have come right out of Willow."[3] And Larry Bossidy, the former chairman and CEO of Honeywell International, writes, "At GE 85 percent of the executives are promoted from within—that's how good the company is at developing leaders."[4]

How to Organize the Team

At this point in building your disciple-making team, we will assume that you have the right people at the right time. The next step is to organize them in a way that best supports and accomplishes your disciple-making process. And you will need a way to communicate this. The questions are, Where in the organization do our people fit? How will they relate to one another? Who is responsible to whom? What exactly is the "pecking order" around here? The answers to these questions involve constructing an organizational chart that visually reflects the church's ministry hierarchy.

The Church's Hierarchy

The corporate world holds that because of change, organizations must be innovative and agile and that rigid, pyramidal organizations do not permit this. And there is some truth to this. Some even mistakenly argue that the best organization is no organization; but people in an organization need to know who is in charge. Peter Drucker writes, "In any institution there has to be a final authority. . . . someone who can make the final decisions and who can expect them to be obeyed. In a situation of common peril—and every institution is likely to encounter it sooner or later—survival of all depends on clear command. . . . It is the only hope in a crisis."[5] In the church context the final authority could be any number of people, depending on the size of the church. In regard to the staff, the person at the top is the senior pastor. He leads the staff, is responsible for hiring and firing the staff, and answers to the board or the congregation, depending on the church's organizational polity.

In addition to knowing who is in charge, the rest of the staff needs to know what their relationships are to one another—who works for whom, what their job is, and to whom they report. This is best represented on a simple organizational chart, especially as the church acquires more staff.

A good job or ministry description will also help clarify and reflect the ministry's organization. For example, at my last church, we needed a minister of Christian education. The man we wanted for the position was most reluctant because we had no job description. He wanted to know all the following regarding this position: What were our performance expectations? Exactly what were his responsibilities? For what would he be held accountable? To whom did he report, and who reported to him? He was wise. The answer for us at the church was to develop a job or ministry description not only for his position but for every working position in the church (I have provided one example of a job description in appendix F).[6]

Span of Control

Another critical area that affects organization is span of control. This concept addresses how many people report to a single leader and is reflected on the organizational chart. This applies not only to the senior pastor but to other primary leadership staff at the lay or professional level. The rule of thumb is that no more than six persons should report to a single leader. And the larger the organization is, the fewer the number of people who report to each leader.[7] My experience has been that most large church pastors have too many people reporting to them. My current church is a megachurch of around six thousand people. Only three staff report directly to the pastor, but he does attempt to interact with the entire staff and other groupings of the staff at least once per month as needed.

How to Deploy the Team

Once you have the right person on the team, you must decide how to deploy him or her. Deployment involves placement, getting the right person in the right place.

Primary Ministry Activities

When you developed your church's disciple-making process, you created a Maturity Matrix that consists of two axes. One is horizontal and reflects the characteristics of a mature disciple. The other, which applies more to staff deployment, is the vertical axis that reflects the church's primary or core ministries, such as a preaching-worship service, a Sunday school, and a small-group ministry. They are the ministry means that accomplish the ends or marks of a mature disciple. You staff to your primary, ordered ministry activities. If you have not determined your primary ministries, then you will need to do so before you can best deploy your ministry people. If you have determined these activities, you are ready to deploy your people.

Staff Champions

You will need to assign a primary staff champion for each—or in some cases several—of your ministries, depending on the number and nature of these activities. For example, the large-group worship meeting is currently a vital and primary ministry that comes early in the assimilation process, at least in Builder and Boomer congregations. There must be a leader, or champion, for this activity. Most likely this will be the senior pastor or lead preacher. It could be a talented, gifted worship leader.

Working through each primary activity, you must determine who is to champion and take responsibility for it. You may have a ratio of one-for-one, or you may have one champion for several activities, as is often the case in church plants and fast-growing churches. The ratio of one-for-one is best, but you may not have the resources to pursue this at present. The important thing is that all the ministry activities are covered. These champions may all be professional people who are on the payroll or, in smaller churches, they will likely be gifted, committed volunteer laypeople.

I should pause briefly to explain the concept of a staff champion. Senior pastors tend to emphasize and even at times overemphasize their areas of passion. For many this is preaching. Other passions might be evangelism and pastoral visitation and care. The problem is that often this emphasis results in the neglect of other vital, primary ministries, and this in turn throws the church off balance. The concept of a staff champion provides someone to "beat the drum" for a primary disciple-making ministry. Each primary ministry has a staff champion who also values the other ministries, which protects from the "silo effect," that is, seeing one's own activity as the most important and practically the only worthwhile activity of the church. Here the staff walk a delicate ministry tightrope, seeking to balance the promotion of their ministry while not creating a silo effect that could be dangerous to the church.

Once you have a staff champion for each of the primary activities, you want to address leadership for other areas. In most churches, this will be provided by talented, committed lay leaders. In addition, as the church grows, you may want to consider some future staff positions, such as a pastor of communications, a web pastor, a pastor of strategic planning, a pastor of stewardship, and so on.

How to Develop the Team

At this point in building your disciple-making team, you have the right person deployed as a champion in the right position who knows where he or she is on the ministry organizational chart. The next step is to plan for his or her development. For staff members this can be at once the most difficult thing about being on a team—and the most rewarding. It has everything to do with working and ministering together in authentic disciple-making community.

So how might you help your staff to grow and develop? The rest of this chapter will answer this question as I explain how to train people in what I refer to as the four core leadership competencies: character, knowledge, skills, and emotions.

It is rumored that more than twenty-five years ago, one of the first army leadership training manuals coined the expression that best summarizes the first three: "Be, know, do." I add a fourth: "feel," which involves the emotions. Achieving excellence in all four competencies must take place for leaders to be able to do their jobs effectively.

The Leader's Character (Being)

Character affects the very heart and soul of the leader as a disciple maker. Though I have already addressed the character issue earlier in this chapter, it bears repeating. It's soul work that develops the leader's Christlikeness from core to crust. Psalm 78:72 says that David shepherded (led) his people with "integrity of heart." America in general and the church in particular is facing a leadership crisis. Leaders must be people of good character. Even the corporate world, after the fall of a number of notable companies (Enron and others), has begun to emphasize the importance of good character and servant leadership. For the church the problem may be in the area of theological education, where it is often assumed that the character development of students has already taken place. Christian educators stress the importance of character development but assume that students are working on this area. This is a poor assumption that has proved fatal for some of our top Christian leaders.

The character component (being) is a leadership competency that demands our attention and development. The importance of character raises the key questions: Who must leaders be to lead effectively at each level of the ministry? What are the character requirements for those who would be disciple makers?

Who do people expect their leaders to be? Scripture provides us with some general character qualities.

As we have already seen, passages such as 1 Timothy 3:1–7; Titus 1:6–9; and 1 Peter 5:2–3 provide the church with the characteristics for elders, who would be equivalent to today's pastors. First Timothy 3:8–13 provides the character qualities for deacons. In 2 Peter 1:3–9 Peter appears to address all Christians with the importance of certain qualities. Acts 6:3–5 provides some qualities for early church leaders, and Galatians 5:22–23 presents the fruit of the Spirit. Some other necessary character qualities are found in 2 Timothy 2:2, such as competence, trustworthiness, and teachability. I consider teachability vital. A lack of teachability is the potential leader's cardinal sin. It quickly disqualifies one from leadership in any area, because leaders must always be learners. Should they stop learning, they stop leading. If one is unteachable at the beginning, he or she is not leadership material.

I encourage leader-trainers to develop character audits to use with their trainees. For those who do not have the time to do so, I have developed two character assessments that are in appendix E, mentioned earlier. One is for male leadership and is based on the character qualities in 1 Timothy 3:1–7 and Titus 1:6–9. The other is for female leadership and is based on 1 Timothy 2:9–10, 3:11; Titus 2:3–5; and 1 Peter 3:1–6. Leader-trainers may find them helpful in assessing the character of those whom they train to be disciple makers.

The Leader's Knowledge (Knowing)

Knowledge impacts the leader's intellect. It's the cognitive aspect of learning that emphasizes the ability to acquire and process content or information. Whether the knowledge is old or newly acquired, leaders must have knowledge of their ministry areas.

In God's preparation of Moses for leadership, he specifically taught him what to do (Exod. 4:15). Competency is based to a great degree on knowing what to do. This is far too often where seminarians come up short in the area of leadership. They are trained well in crucial areas such as the languages, theology, church history, and preaching, but receive little training, if any, in leadership. A seminary colleague once said that his biggest struggle when he was a pastor-leader was knowing what to do.

The key questions regarding the leader's knowledge are: What must one know to lead at his or her level of this ministry? What are the basic knowledge requirements to lead in one's area of disciple making or expertise? Those responsible for developing leaders who train and make disciples in the various core ministries must carve time out of their busy schedules to answer these crucial questions.

To identify all the knowledge components for leaders in the primary disciple-making ministries is beyond the scope of this book. That information would fill several books. But the following should get you started in thinking this through.

Leaders who make disciples must know God (Romans 6–8).

They must know themselves (their divine design, strengths, and weaknesses).

They must know people (this involves knowing how to use tools, such as the Personal Profile and the Kiersey Temperament Sorter for training purposes).

They should know how to study the Bible and have a general knowledge of the Bible and theology.

They should know how to pray.

They must know and agree with the organization's statements (core values, mission, vision, strategy, and beliefs or doctrine).

They need to know how to think and plan strategically.

They need to have a theology of discipleship, which means they understand what the Bible says about making disciples (see chapters 5 and 6).

They must know what it takes to make disciples in their areas of ministry, whether worship and preaching, small-group ministries, the Sunday school program, ABF (Adult Bible Fellowship) program, or any other ministries that are the church's primary ministries for making disciples.

And senior pastors should know how to preach, raise money, and develop staff.

The Leader's Skills (Doing)

The disciple-making leader's skills affect the leader's actions or behavior. I referred to Psalm 78:72, which states that David led his people with "integrity of heart." It also says that he led them with "skillful hands." Leaders must be able to put into practice what they learn. They may have leadership knowledge, but can they lead in their primary ministries? Can they turn theory into practice?

The key skills questions are: What must one be able to do to lead a disciple-making ministry? What skills must one have to function well in one's area of leadership? What habits are necessary for effective leadership and ministry? Leaders in each core disciple-making ministry must answer these questions for the people they train.

Leaders should be aware of both task skills and relational skills that are needed for ministry. Hard or task skills include casting vision, praying, discovering and developing core ministry values, developing a ministry mission statement and strategy, and ability to teach and preach the Bible or a Sunday school lesson. I have listed these in a Task Skills Inventory in appendix H that you can use with developing leaders. The soft or relational skills include listening, encouraging, mentoring or coaching, resolving conflicts, networking, counseling, motivating, taking risks, solving problems, and building trust. A Relational Skills Inventory can be found in appendix G.

The Leader's Emotions (Feeling)

Simply stated, your emotions are your feelings. The disciple-making leader's emotions are their heart-work, reflecting what they feel. Scripture has much to say about emotions, beginning in Genesis when Adam and Eve experienced shame due to their sin (Gen. 3:7 compared to Gen. 2:25) and extending through Revelation where John, describing the New Jerusalem, writes, "He will wipe every tear from their eyes. There will be no more death or mourning or crying or pain, for the old order of things has passed away" (Rev. 21:4).

Leaders' emotions affect their mood. And research as well as ministry experience tells us that the leaders' mood is most contagious, spreading quickly throughout a ministry. A good mood characterized by optimism and inspiration affects people positively. A bad mood characterized by negativity and pessimism will cripple the ministry and damage existing and potential disciples.

The key emotions questions for leaders who would make disciples are: What emotions are liabilities for your primary ministry? What emotions must you deal with to create a better climate for that ministry? Again, it is beyond the scope of this book to go into great detail regarding the leader's emotions. The following overview should help catalyze your thinking in this area.

To develop emotional well-being and establish a spiritually healthy climate for their primary ministry, leaders must deal with their own emotions and those of the people with whom and to whom they minister.

THE LEADER'S EMOTIONS

Leaders must understand and then manage their own emotions. This involves taking four steps:

Step 1: Leaders must learn to recognize their emotions when they occur.

Step 2: They should learn to identify their emotions, such as anger, anxiety, sadness, fear, shame, discouragement, surprise, joy, and love.

Step 3: They must begin to deal with their emotions.

Step 4: Leaders may want to explore the reason they're experiencing certain emotions.

Once leaders begin to understand their emotions, step 3 involves managing their emotions. To accomplish this, they need to remember two things.

- We can't control being swept up by our emotions, because often the emotional mind overrides the rational mind, such as when we lose our temper.

- We can control how we respond to or handle our emotions when they occur. We can recognize them and deal biblically with them in the power of the Holy Spirit.

Step 4 encourages leaders to attempt to get at the causes for certain emotions. For example, if a person feels anxiety or anger, he or she would be wise to try to identify the circumstances or thoughts behind these feelings. And working with a counselor might prove helpful.

The Emotions of Others

Leaders must not only be aware of and work on their own emotions but also recognize others' emotions and help them to manage these emotions as well.

This is commonly referred to as empathy. Most of us have been in situations where an emotionally unhealthy person, whether in a leadership position or not, affects a ministry context negatively. It is imperative that leaders deal with these people for the sake of the ministry as well as the individual. Leaders accomplish this in much the same way as they work with their own emotions, applying the four steps to others. This can be done by example and by working one-on-one, using the same approach to help others manage their emotions as leaders use with their own.

The assumption here is that people in or under our primary disciple-making ministries want help dealing with their emotions. The problem is that the person needing help is often emotionally and spiritually dysfunctional and not willing to work on the issues. The leader should attempt to work with such a person but should also be ready to get professional help for him or her if needed. If the staff person refuses such help or shows little progress, then it is time to let him or her go.

Leader's Developed Capabilities	
Character (being)	Soul-work
Knowledge (knowing)	Headwork
Skills (doing)	Handwork
Emotions (feeling)	Heart-work

The Need for Balanced Leadership Development

Having briefly explained the four core leadership competencies—character, knowledge, skills, and emotions—I now want to attach a warning label to what I have said. A distortion in learning can happen if we emphasize any one of the elements over the others. Character is a must, but without knowledge and skills it severely limits one's ministry. The leader is a nice guy but doesn't know what he is doing. Knowledge without skills is dry intellectualism. Again, this is a major problem in our seminaries where faculty and students can be disconnected from the real world of the church and much learning is merely theoretical. A skill without knowledge is mindless activity or mere busywork, and skills without character can lead to mere task-oriented ministry. Finally, emotions without knowledge lead to frustration. The leader knows something is wrong but does not know what it is or how to get relief. Good leader-teachers train their emerging leaders to integrate and balance as much as possible the four competencies in their disciple-making ministries.

Questions for Reflection and Discussion

1. Do you agree with the author's view that a church will only be as good as the people who make up the disciple-making team? Why or why not?

2. Do you prefer a team or "lone ranger" approach to ministry? Why? Take a moment and reflect on your past ministry experience. Has it been a team or a lone ranger approach? Why? Which does the New Testament support?

3. Are you in a position where you can choose people who should be on your disciple-making team, or are the members of your team those who happen to be available or already on the team? If the latter, what can or will you do about this?

4. Do you agree with the author's definition of a staff team? Why or why not?

5. Ministry silos are ministry killers. Are there any silos among your disciple-making ministries? If so, why are they there and what do you plan to do about them?

6. Do you have the luxury of recruiting staff before it is clear to all that you need them? If not, what is your philosophy of recruitment? Do you have enough staff based on the chart that compares the number of staff to average worship attendance?

7. Is your current staff balanced between age-specific and functional ministries? Are they balanced between outreach and in-reach? If not, which is predominant? Do they complement one another? Why or why not?

8. How does your current staff fare when you critique them with the three Cs (character, competence, and chemistry)? Do they align with your values, mission, vision, and disciple-making strategy? Are they committed to the latter? If not, why? What will you do about this?

9. Do you think that in your situation it is best to recruit people from outside or inside the church? Why? What has the church practiced in the past? Why?

10. Do you currently have staff champions for your disciple-making ministries? If not, why not? What will you do about this?

11. Do you have an organizational chart? Do you have ministry descriptions for any current staff people? Why or why not? If not, what will you do about it?

12. Do you have in place a process to develop your leaders, especially those who lead and are involved in your key disciple-making ministries? Why or why not? The author suggests you train them in four leadership competencies. Do you agree? Do you find the information about these four competencies helpful? Will training in these areas work in your situation? Why or why not?

11

How to Prepare
a Strategic Budget

Budgeting for the Development of Mature Disciples

If you have been in ministry for a while, you know that it costs a lot of money to operate a church. Bill Hybels writes, "Be as theological as you want to be, but the church will never reach her full redemptive potential until a river of financial sources starts flowing in her direction."[1] However, few churches in the early twenty-first century have an abundance of money for ministry. Expenses and expectations are up while contributions are down. The church is primarily dependent on the support of its people for survival. In most situations, one out of three adult attenders donates nothing to the church, and those who do contribute, give less than 3 percent of their aggregate income, despite Jesus's warning in Matthew 6:21: "For where your treasure is, there your heart will be also."

This chapter will address how to prepare a strategic budget to make disciples. As a consultant, I can tell what a church truly values by looking at a copy of the budget, because most churches spend their money on what they value most. In this book you have learned that your disciple-making ministries are critical to the mission and vision of your church, and this must be reflected in your budget.

The Responsibility for Raising Ministry Funding

So who is responsible for raising the ministry's finances? Let me give the rest of what Bill Hybels writes, which I quoted above: "Be as theological as you want to be, but the church will never reach her full redemptive potential until a river of financial sources starts flowing in her direction. *And like it or not, it is the leader's job to create that river and to manage it wisely. The sooner the leader realizes that the better.*"[2]

Most pastors do not like to raise finances, but the truth is that they, not some board or committee, are responsible for the church's finances in general and raising them in particular. Each semester I can anticipate the shocked look on my students' faces when I inform them of this pastoral leadership "fact of life." And I know what they are thinking: *I have committed to go into the ministry to teach and preach the Scriptures, not to raise and manage money!* When congregational push comes to shove, though, the church looks to no one else but the pastor to take responsibility for its finances. Literally, the buck stops with him.

Regardless of how you feel about it, if you are the leader of your congregation, you are responsible for raising its finances. Thus an important first step is accepting this fact.

A Biblical View

Scripture is not entirely clear on the issue of raising funds for the church. Paul seems to have been involved unapologetically in raising finances for himself (Phil. 4:10–20 and possibly 1 Cor. 9:11–12) and for churches (2 Corinthians 8–9). But he was an apostle and more a church planter than a pastor, at least in today's sense. I believe that the first-century pastors were likely the elders or overseers, and little is said about their management of finances, and what is said is not entirely clear. I hold that leaders are responsible for raising funds for the following reasons.

First, Paul provides us with a list of the qualifications to be an overseer or pastor of a first-century house church. In 1 Timothy 3:4–5 he writes, "He must manage his own family well and see that his children obey him with proper respect. (If anyone does not know how to manage his own family, how can he take care of God's church?)" Here Paul uses an obvious analogy between how one manages his family and the church. Though he does not go into particulars, I would think that providing for one's family has to include finances. Consequently, the same would hold for the elder's management of the church.

Next, in 1 Timothy 5:17 he writes, "The elders who direct the affairs of the church well are worthy of double honor, especially those whose work is preaching and teaching." Here he notes that a function of these first-century pastors was to "direct the affairs of the church," and funding was needed to do ministry, just as it is today. I suspect that "directing the affairs of the church" included raising the necessary funding. In these situations where Scripture is not prescriptive, or in this case specific, I believe the church has freedom to decide these issues (see 2 Cor. 3:17). The pastor's responsibility for raising the necessary funding has been a part of the church's culture for a long time and likely will not change anytime soon.

A Challenge

But rather than viewing the need to manage funds as a curse, why not view it as a challenge? In my years as a pastor, I viewed it as a necessary drudgery. Recently I asked myself why. The answer was that I knew so little about money and had trouble even balancing my own checkbook. All that changed as I began to learn more about the funding side of ministry and how it is ultimately God's work, not mine. In time I have come to view it as a stewardship challenge— to help people see the importance of stewardship in their lives and the life of the church in making disciples. In addition, I have discovered that raising finances is not all that difficult when you know what you are doing and are willing to trust God for his provisions. Thus I have changed my mind about managing money in the church. My challenge to leaders is to lead in the area of your church's finances, embracing this responsibility and accepting it as a challenge from the Lord.

The Board's Responsibility

The responsibility of the church board in fund-raising and fund management is to assign these tasks to the senior pastor. I think that it is important to say this, because my experience in smaller churches is that this is more assumed than assigned. And this may be true in larger churches as well. The board's role will be to monitor, not micromanage, the pastor's fund-raising and fund management through such means as monthly financial reports and updates.

The Pastor's Responsibility

Though the pastor has full responsibility for raising funds and then seeing that they are properly managed, that does not imply that he has to do it all himself. There are times when he might get help from others in the congregation. However, the church does not need any unsupervised, "renegade" fund-raisers, especially staff who are out raising funds for their disciple-making ministries. Any help from others must be coordinated with and through the pastor. And he would be wise to get some help in managing the money that he has raised. For most of us there is little enjoyment in number crunching, but the larger churches may have a business administrator or manager or in some rare cases a pastor of stewardship who with an accountant or two will manage the funds and make reports to the pastor. Smaller churches can solicit volunteer help from laypeople who work with finances for a living.

Even with the help of those with financial expertise, it is the responsibility of the pastor to oversee the finances. Who else besides the senior pastor could take this role in the church? In our culture people look to the leader for direction and inspiration in church funding. It is part of their package of cultural expectations. That is one of the many hats that the pastor wears. While they must be strongly supportive, a board chairperson, an executive pastor, an assistant pastor, a pastor of finances or stewardship, even a church patriarch or matriarch cannot perform the role of fund manager. In evangelical churches most people realize that the Bible says much about stewardship, and it is the pastor who knows the Bible best and is responsible to communicate this information to them. The responsibility falls on his shoulders naturally. If the senior pastor is not good at or willing to assume this function, the church is in trouble and will struggle financially.

Why do pastors in general shy away from the financial side of the ministry? I suspect that there are at least three reasons.

1. *They do not know how to manage money.* It is rare that money management is ever addressed in seminary, and we tend to shy away from what we do not know. Still, finances must be raised if the ministry is to thrive. So the solution is to learn how to do it and lead the church in the area of its finances. The best approach is to find a pastor who is most competent at fund management and ask him to teach you how to do it. There are also a few good books out on the topic, and I recommend *Money Matters in Church*,[3] which I wrote with my pastor, Steve Stroope, who is a genius in the area of raising and managing church finances.

2. *Pastors worry too much about offending people* over money or leaving the impression that all they are interested in is people's money for their own gain. They assume mistakenly that it is a sore spot with their people, who they think will criticize them if they ask for their money. What they fail to realize is that the people in the congregation who complain the most about giving money are the ones who are not supporting the church well with their finances. And when the pastor preaches on the topic, they feel convicted about what they are not doing. Then pastors worry about visitors—what will they think? So they never broach the topic of the funding for ministry.

3. *They are concerned about their self-image.* Many people have grown up in situations where they had enough money and never had to ask for any. Thus, asking people to give affects the pastor's personal es-

teem. He believes wrongly that people will view him as they do the televangelists—motivated more by money than ministry.

One of the reasons that I give my Church Giving Inventory to congregations with whom I consult is that, among other reasons, it addresses this pastoral self-image issue. So far I have not found a congregation whose response to fund-raising is negative, so pastors' fears are unfounded. Actually, congregations want to hear more about finances in general and to know what the Bible says in particular. I assume there are exceptions, but I have not come across one. When the pastors I work with hear this from the congregation, it has a major positive impact on their esteem and attitude toward raising ministry funding.

The Staff's Responsibility

The disciple-making staff has several responsibilities. Here are three:

1. To operate with integrity within its budget.
2. To assist the pastor where needed and when requested.
3. To be "cash sensitive," which means being aware that their actions either use or generate cash.

Should disciple-making staff raise funds, especially for their ministry areas? This should not be a requirement; if some have the ability, this could be done under the direction of the pastor. And some churches might consider hiring a pastor of stewardship to assist and work closely with the senior pastor in the fund-raising effort.

The Results of Ignoring Giving

One problem with not addressing giving, at least biblical giving and raising finances, is that it has the effect of denigrating stewardship. It gives people permission not to give and to rationalize not doing so. This is not allowed in other areas of the Christian life. If we knew that people in our congregation were having a problem with gossip, would we not address it? And would we apologize for preaching on it, as some leaders do when they preach about finances? While we are more interested in people's souls than their pocketbooks, we have to teach and preach about their pocketbooks, because we are most interested in their souls.

Another problem with not addressing giving is that the church comes up short of the funds necessary to support what the church is supposed to be doing—making disciples. Without proper, generous support, these ministries will operate with a pronounced limp. And ultimately, few if any will be satisfied with the results.

How Much Money Should Be Raised?

Since the pastor is the one the church expects to raise its funding, how much does he need to raise? The formal answer to this question is found in the church's budget. The budget provides the general funding goal or target for the fund-raising pastor, unless the church is also involved in some special program, such as a capital funds project that goes beyond the budget.

I believe that a church that desires biblical, numerical growth, such as we see in Acts (Acts 1:15; 2:41; 4:4; 5:14; 6:1; 9:31; 11:21, 24; 14:1, 21; 16:5; 17:4, 12; 18:8, 10; 19:26; 21:20), assigns a percentage of funds to four key areas: missions and evangelism, personnel, programming, and facilities. All of these contribute in some way to fulfilling the church's mission and vision to make disciples.

Missions and Evangelism

Most churches realize the importance of and the need to support missions to some extent. I like to include evangelism here as well because some, such as the Builder generation, tend to replace evangelism, especially evangelism in their immediate community, with writing a check to missions. Both missions and evangelism should be priorities of the church.

I believe that a church that desires biblical, numerical growth in terms of disciples will budget around 10 percent for missions and evangelism. This sends a clear message that they value or desire to value evangelism and missions. This, however, is just a starting place. It should not be all that the church gives in this area. I challenge every church to raise additional funds for missions and evangelism and make it a part of any capital funds project.

Someone might ask, why make missions and evangelism separate from the ministries for making disciples that are found under programming? The answer is that, while they are to work together, missions and evangelism need an emphasis all of their own. As I consult with churches from border to border and coast to coast, I find very few that value evangelism, and both evangelism and missions are critical to any church that wants to live and breathe disciple making. Thus, providing a separate place in the budget for missions and evangelism puts special emphasis on them and sends a message that they are vital to the church that makes disciples.

Personnel

The section for ministry personnel in the budget is vital to the church's making disciples, and it is the largest allocation of funds in most budgets, because people need to be properly supported. Therefore, I recommend that the church designate around 50 percent of its budget to its personnel, most of whom are involved in some way in its disciple-making ministries. Often in larger churches it is a little less and in smaller churches a little more.

Why so much? You will recall from the prior chapter the importance of staffing. People are God's human agents for ministry effectiveness. He could do it himself through miracles, but he prefers to accomplish his purposes through people (Phil. 2:13) and then blesses them in return. Your disciple-making ministry will only be as good as the people who serve the Lord and the church. While there may be a few ministers who are out to fleece the flock or to make lots of money, Scripture is clear that the worker (in this context, likely, the first-century pastor) deserves his wages (1 Tim. 5:17–18). In fact, Paul says those who lead well and preach and teach are worthy of double honor. It is not only unbiblical but shameful when a church that has the means fails to take care of its workers. Many of us have heard the stories of church power struggles when a particular group of people withhold their tithes and offerings in an attempt to "starve out" the pastor. This carnal behavior serves only to shame the Savior, invites God's discipline on these people and possibly the church, and paralyzes the church's disciple-making efforts.

To use its funds wisely, the church should have personnel policies in place that address staff finances. These should establish what a base salary should be and how to handle raises. Are there automatic cost-of-living raises? Are raises granted regardless of performance, or are raises strictly based on performance?

Programming

A church must pay careful attention to its programming, because this is how it serves God and directly funds its disciple-making ministries. It also has a major impact on fund-raising, as people contribute through the various disciple-making church ministries. I suggest that a church put approximately 20 to 25 percent of its funding into programming.

The major part of programming is the church's primary ministry activities that I covered earlier in this book. You listed these on the vertical axis of the Maturity Matrix. And the church will focus on funding the primary ministries, not its secondary ministries, as they are so key to making mature disciples. In addition, some of them, such as the worship service, will provide the greatest funding in return. For example, in terms of ROI (return on investment), the worship service provides for much of the church's income and will likely fund the rest of the primary ministry activities.

The church will also need to consider its people's programming expectations. For example, some people believe that, because they support the church financially, it should, in turn, provide them with Sunday school supplies and other personal materials that may be a part of the program. The thinking is that we give to the church and expect something in return rather than we give to the Lord and will pay for our own personal ministry needs.

Facilities

Another area that affects the church's disciple-making ministries is the church's setting, which consists of its location and facilities. Every church has a site and location where it makes disciples. Here I want to focus specifically on its facilities. Well-meaning church planters will often start out their ministries with the idea that they will invest in people rather than bricks and mortar. This means that they do not plan to purchase or build a facility. Their plan is to rent what they need and put the rest back into recruiting and securing competent staff who are key to their disciple-making vision. While this sounds great, unfortunately it never works quite that way. I suspect that a part of it is culture. People want a place they can identify with and call their own ("our church"). They also grow weary of all the disadvantages of not owning a building, such as unclean facilities and setting up and taking down chairs and tables. The bottom line is that in time most churches embrace the need for a permanent facility.

I suggest that a church allocate around 20 to 25 percent of its budget for facilities. This would include primarily a mortgage payment and maintenance. I have worked with at least one church that had paid off its mortgage and, therefore, diverted the mortgage amount from facilities to another part of the budget. I would not recommend that a church do this. The reason is that when the funds are designated for another part of the budget, it eliminates the church's ability to service any future notes for building purposes. If, due to growth, the church needs to add to or extensively renovate the current facilities, there will be no funds budgeted for that purpose, and the cost of renovations or an addition would either be impossible to cover or would place a huge strain on the current budget.

If you really plan to grow and make more disciples, whether or not you have a mortgage, you are wise to create a building fund and let people have an opportunity to give to it as well as to other parts of the ministry.

How Is Money Raised?

As I said above, I am convinced that many leaders would focus more on raising finances for making disciples if they knew how. Therefore, in this section I want to address several means that pastors can use to raise the ministry's operational finances that fund the budget and encourage and support its disciple-making ministries.

A Biblical Theology of Finances

First, you must be able to articulate a biblical theology of finances. I believe that the pastor should have thought through what he believes the Bible teaches about finances and stewardship and should write down his views. Any biblical directives should be incorporated into his views. What does the Old Testament teach us about giving? What does Christ teach us in the Gospels? What do the Epistles teach? For example, what about tithing? Does a mature disciple have to tithe? If so, how much is a tithe, and where does Scripture support this?

The pastor will also need to preach and teach on giving, and he must have a biblical theology to do so. My pastor, Steve Stroope, and I included a biblical theology of finances in appendix A of our book *Money Matters in Church*.

The Church's Disciple-Making Vision

The pastor must regularly cast the church's compelling vision for making and maturing disciples. The key to raising finances for your church's ministry is vision. My experience is that people are not that interested in paying the light bills or staff salaries, nor do they respond well to guilt trips, negativism, or needs. People give to big, dynamic visions that, in turn, produce passion that is vital to giving. They are more willing to invest in "what could be" (future possibilities) than "what is" (present reality), especially if "what is" is floundering or in the red. The exception is when "what is" is obviously blessed of God and growing spiritually and numerically.

To a certain degree, raising finances is a measure of the church's vision. People's giving response will often tell you something about the quality of your church's vision and the leader's ability to cast that vision. The only way people can really know the church's vision is through the vision caster and how that person articulates and frames it in the context of disciple making. A pastor who fails to or cannot cast vision will have a negative impact on the church's income and ultimately its mission. Hopefully, you have a vision in place. What remains is for you to communicate it well and over and over in every way possible. Should you need some help with the vision, see my book *Developing a Vision for Ministry in the Twenty-first Century*.[4]

A Churchwide Stewardship Ministry

The pastor must implement a churchwide stewardship ministry. Of these six means for raising finances, I believe that this is the most important. Scripture has much to say about giving, and this forms the biblical basis for your stewardship ministries that support disciple making. You must develop and implement a strategy for building biblical stewardship into your ministry. To do this, certain ministry activities (the means) that will assist your people in becoming mature givers (the ends) are essential. I strongly encourage you to implement all of the following activities in your church as part of your stewardship ministry.

SERMONS

It is imperative that pastors and teaching teams communicate what the Bible says about giving. It is a key part of making mature disciples. As already noted, some shirk this responsibility, fearing what their people or visitors might think. Many pastors want to please their people and be liked. That is normal; however, a significant difference exists between being liked and being respected. Jesus did not hesitate to address people in the area of their finances (see, for example, Matt. 6:19–24), and pastors would be wise to follow his example. My experience is that most people really do want to know what the Bible teaches about money because it is an issue that is so close to their hearts. Many know that their finances are not providing true happiness, and they want to know the truth. People of God must know the Word of God, and pastors must be truth tellers.

Some pastors set aside one month each year for positive, motivating biblical instruction on giving. Barna's research argues that pastors who preach two or more messages in a series usually receive a better response than those who preach only once a year or several messages spread out over the year.[5] I suggest that you approach your messages along the lines that giving is a privilege as much as it is a responsibility. Resist the temptation to bang the congregation over the head with biblical imperatives. Instead, assume that they want to give and you are there to instruct and help them enjoy the privilege of giving to God.

SUNDAY SCHOOL

A core disciple-making ministry in many churches is the Sunday school. Take three or four sessions annually in your Sunday school or ABF ministry to cover some aspect of stewardship. An example could be a series entitled "Managing Your Money God's Way." These studies could be coordinated with stewardship sermons or at a different time of the year. If Sunday school follows the worship time, an alternative is to discuss the meaning of the sermon on finances or giving and ways to apply what has been taught.

SMALL GROUPS

Another key disciple-making ministry in churches is a small-group program. If you have small-group ministries along with or in place of a Sunday school, involve them in a Bible study on giving. They could follow up the sermon with discussion and application. Another good option for small groups might be a twelve-week study on finances, using material from an organization such as Crown Financial Ministries (www.crown.org).

New Members Class

A time when people are most interested in and committed to the church and its ministry is when they decide to join it. Wise churches provide a new members or partners class to orient them to the church. It is critical that they cover matters such as the church's values, mission, vision, and disciple-making strategy to align new members with the church's program. And this is also a great time for the church to communicate its giving expectations and the biblical basis for them.

Counseling

Along with the various ministries that teach about biblical giving, the church will need to provide some counseling for those who are struggling with debt and other financial problems. The church could set up a financial fitness center that helps people address any debt, establish personal budgets, and pursue financial planning. It is likely that there are several people in a congregation who are good with finances and others who are counselors. These individuals could team together to help those who struggle financially.

Ministry of Deferred Giving

Early in the twenty-first century there are more affluent people than ever before, and many of them are members of our churches. While most have estate plans, they have not included the church in them. I would argue that the church has a responsibility to inform them of the opportunity to have a lasting impact on the church through estate giving. I advise all pastors to search their congregations for retired or currently active individuals who have worked in estate planning or are CFPs (certified financial planners) and could lead this ministry on a volunteer basis. A larger congregation might want to have a pastor of finances or stewardship or generosity (as some are calling it today) who leads such a ministry.

Workshops and Seminars

The church should consider offering quarterly or semiannual workshops on some aspects of giving, such as budgeting, investing, estate planning, retirement, and many other similar topics of interest. Call it Biblical Money Management 101 and 102 or some other name. In addition, consider inviting unchurched people in the community to attend, providing them with a positive, practical exposure to the church.

Constantly Communicating with the Congregation

It is imperative that a disciple-making church communicate constantly with its congregation. People whom leaders keep in the dark, for whatever reason, will not trust their leaders. If the congregation does not trust the leaders, they will not follow them. The same holds true for raising finances. If the congregation does not trust the leaders, they will not give. Why would they contribute their money to those whom they do not trust? Thus, if you are having problems raising funds, ask yourself, *Does the congregation trust the leadership?*

Constant communication says we have nothing to hide and creates a sense of ownership that inevitably invites people to support the ministry. You tend to support that which is yours. Barna writes, "Remember: people cannot own a ministry they do not understand, and people cannot understand it if they are not kept up to date about its status."[6]

You can practice constant communication both informally and formally. Encourage the leadership or any others who might be spearheading a campaign or the regular weekly administration of funds to share with people what is going on. You can communicate formally through one-way methods, such as bulletins, newsletters, personal letters, video announcements and testimonies, skits, and public testimonies from your good givers. Two-way methods include online chat rooms, town hall meetings, personal telephone calls, and listening groups.

Capital Funds Campaigns

I strongly encourage churches to conduct regular capital campaigns to fund special projects, such as missions giving, the purchase of property, new construction, facility relocation, facility renovation, debt reduction, annual budget campaigns, and other key projects that require monies over and above the general fund. Though missions should already be included in the budget, you would be wise to raise additional support to expand your missions network. In general, people support and seem always to find more money for missions.

An average campaign should raise one and a half to two times the church's annual undesignated offerings, paid out over a three-year period. An excellent campaign will raise three times as much. The campaign itself usually lasts three to five months, and pledges will come in over the following three years. Perhaps the best time to begin a campaign is January, because there are fewer outside pressures on people's time and personal finances at that time.

What I like so much about these campaigns is that they serve to provide a necessary "kick in the pants" to promote sacrificial giving on our part. Though most of you reading this book give well, you, like me, could do even better. We need an occasional prod or reminder to give a little extra.

A number of larger churches are using fund-raising organizations to conduct capital campaigns for them because they do not know how to do it on their own. This is wise, and many of these churches report that after the campaign, general giving remains higher than before. Churches should consider using a fund-raising organization as a viable option. There are a number of organizations that are most helpful in planning and executing these special campaigns, but be sure to check out the organization first. Ask for references and contact them personally. Of course, I highly recommend the Malphurs Group for this service.

Giving Champions

You should identify those in your church with the gift of giving. Rather than ignoring them as many pastors are inclined to do, meet with them periodically and cultivate their gift along with their relationship with God as you might someone with the gifts of leadership, evangelism, or preaching. Ask how the church can minister effectively to them and help them to become reproducing disciples. Do not forget to thank them for their ministry to the church. Make sure that they understand the church's mission, vision, and strategy for making disciples. There may be times when you will ask them to consider exercising their gift for a particular cause, such as missions or a new facility. That is okay, because we expect leaders to lead, evangelists to evangelize, and preachers to preach. Why should we not expect givers to give? It is easier to ask for gifts if you have already developed a disciple-making relationship with them. They may also help you to reach out to others who may also have the gift of giving.

I realize that this is controversial and questionable to some; however, if we attempt to cultivate the other gifts of our people, why ignore this one? A *Leadership* journal article interviewed four pastors on how they handle finances in their churches. All four knew who their gifted givers were and at times asked them for financial help.[7] The key here is motive. Are you seeking funds for your own personal benefit? This cannot really be an issue when the money is not necessarily going to support the pastor's salary, or does so only indirectly, along with supporting a number of special, worthy projects. Motive of the pastor is usually not an issue unless there is a low degree of trust in the church leadership.

To cultivate giving champions, you must know how much your people give. This is also controversial for some pastor-leaders, because it involves their access to the congregation's giving records. Jesus makes it clear that where our treasure is, there our hearts will be also (Matt. 6:21). If a pastor needs to know who his mature disciples are, the acid test is likely their giving. This would not only be true in raising funds but in raising up leaders in other areas, such as in selecting board members, potential disciple-making staff, and other critical positions. Rather than knowing how much individuals are giving, some pastors rely on a bookkeeper or financial secretary to tell them who the gifted givers are.

How Is Money Raised?

1. Articulate a biblical theology of finances.
2. Regularly cast the church's disciple-making vision.
3. Implement a churchwide stewardship ministry.
   Sermons
   Sunday school
   Small groups
   New members class
   Counseling
   Ministry of deferred giving
   Workshops and seminars
4. Constantly communicate with the congregation.
5. Conduct capital funds campaigns.
6. Cultivate giving champions.

Questions for Reflection and Discussion

1. Who in your church is primarily responsible for raising finances? Is it the pastor? As far as you know, has this always been the case? Is this biblical? If it is the pastor, how well is he doing? What does this responsibility entail?

2. How do you respond to the assumption that the pastor is responsible to raise the church's finances? Honestly, if you are the pastor, do you view it as a challenge or a curse? If the latter, why? How might you grow and change to view it as a challenge? Why would you not want to lead your church in the area of its finances?

3. What are the key areas for allocation in your budget? Does the budget break down into the areas the author recommends for growing, healthy, disciple-making churches? If not, where does it differ? Do the percentages for each area line up with those the author suggests? How might you change your current budget to reflect the information covered in the budgeting section of this chapter? If you feel that you want to make some of these changes but cannot, what is the problem?

4. Have you articulated a biblical theology of stewardship? If so, is it written down on paper? If not, you do not have one. Why is it so important to your ministry?

5. Does the section in this chapter on raising finances make sense? What do you agree with, and what do you struggle with the most? If you are the pastor, do you feel competent to lead a capital funds campaign? Why or why not? If not, what will you do? Are you comfortable with bringing in outside expertise? Why or why not?

6. What are your feelings about cultivating your champions (gifted givers)? Will you pursue this? Why or why not? Are you comfortable with having access to the giving records of your people? Why or why not?

Appendix A

Pastoral Care and the Role of the Pastor

Over the past few years, God has allowed me not only to teach leadership at Dallas Seminary but also to minister in numerous churches and denominations as a consultant and trainer. As I work with various leaders, I've come across a fundamental assumption on which some base their pastoral paradigm. It's the assumption that the primary and foremost role of the pastor is to provide pastoral care for the congregation—to take care of the sheep. This would include such hands-on care as visitation in the hospital and at home, counseling, and care during a crisis.

I challenge this assumption both biblically (exegetically) and practically. I believe that while pastoral care is a function of the pastorate, it's neither the primary nor the foremost role of the pastor. The primary responsibility of the pastor is to lead the congregation, which includes such things as teaching the Scriptures, propagating the mission, casting a vision, strategizing to accomplish the church's mission, protecting the sheep from false teaching, and other functions.

Both the Old Testament and the New Testament use shepherd imagery of leaders, but a study of such passages reveals that this imagery refers to leadership more than to pastoral care.

We begin with an examination of the shepherd metaphor in the Old Testament. While pastoral care may have been an aspect of what some leaders in the Old Testament did, their primary role was that of leadership. For example, the prophets and God commonly used the term *shepherd* of the political leaders of

Israel and the nations (2 Sam. 7:7; Isa. 44:28; Jer. 25:34–38; and Ezek. 34:1–4). The emphasis here is clearly on them as leaders. In Psalm 78:70–72 the psalmist writes of David as Israel's shepherd. Is he referring here to David as the primary caregiver or leader of the nation? The answer is found in verse 72, where he uses parallelism. First, he says that David shepherded Israel "with integrity of heart." Then he follows with a parallel statement, "with skillful hands he led them." The latter term *led* explains the former *shepherded*. We see much the same in 2 Samuel 5:2, where the Israelites said to David, "And the LORD said to you, 'You will shepherd my people Israel, and you will become their ruler.'" From these verses we can conclude that, whether or not these leaders provided some type of pastoral care, the main thrust of what they did was to lead people.

In the New Testament Jesus picks up on this imagery and uses it about himself, emphasizing specifically his leadership (John 10:1–6, 27). Then others such as Luke (Acts 20:28–29) and Peter (1 Peter 5:1–4) use it of the leaders in the church. These passages emphasize the role of the shepherd-leader as protector, overseer, and example to the flock.

Another point that relies less on shepherd imagery but is important to this discussion is found in Acts 6:1–7. The apostles and the early church found themselves in a difficult situation in which one group of members was complaining that the other group was neglecting their widows—definitely a pastoral care situation. It's important to note how the apostles handled it. They delegated the pastoral care responsibility (the care of the widows) to others rather than doing it themselves. And the reason is most important, "We will turn this responsibility over to them and will give our attention to prayer and the ministry of the word" (vv. 3–4). If pastoral care is the most important function, then why didn't they say so? Instead, they indicate that prayer and the ministry of the Word were most important.

There are several practical reasons for being careful about overemphasizing the pastoral care side of a pastor's ministry. Research teaches us that some pastors who are strong in pastoral care tend to resist healthy, necessary growth in their churches, because if the church adds more people through evangelism or some other means, it will grow too big for the pastor to be able to care for all the people. This puts an unreasonable demand on his time. He wonders, *How can I visit and care for all these people whom I love? There aren't enough hours in the day.* Thus, often unconsciously, he resists healthy growth, and the church stays small in size and fails to reach lost people.

Another reason is that, whether pastoral care is overemphasized or not, some in the church, often the older members, expect the pastor to visit them, particularly when they're in the hospital. If he fails to visit them for even a legitimate reason, they may be offended. This promotes the false idea that if the pastor doesn't visit you, then you haven't been visited.

This leads to a third reason. Others in the congregation may have gifts in the pastoral care area (Ephesians 4:11 applies to laypeople as well as pastoral leaders!) and will often use these gifts when visiting people in the hospital. But if the pastor tries to do all the visiting, the laypeople aren't able to exercise their gifts of pastoral care. This diminishes and even discourages this important ministry of the laity in the church.

Some ministries in the church may be better at providing pastoral care than the pastor, who may not be gifted in this area. For example, one of the advantages of a small-group ministry is that it provides hands-on pastoral care for its members. I recall visiting one of the ladies in my church who was in the hospital. When I arrived, I found several of the people in her small group there ministering to and caring for her. I suspect that I was more in their way than a help to her.

Finally, some churches are too large for the pastor to visit and offer pastoral care to all or even some of the members. How, then, can his role be primarily that of pastoral care? If it is, then we should demand that he visit everybody.

Based on the New Testament, I believe that other leadership functions are more important to the church than pastoral care. One example is helping the church to develop and adopt a passionate, compelling mission statement. The Savior gave the church its mission statement—to make and mature disciples—in Matthew 28:19–20. This is what the church is to be about. And the way to evaluate the effectiveness of the church is to look for its disciples. Do you want to know if your church is effective? Look for disciples! While the Great Commission includes pastoral care, it's much broader than that.

We may wonder where this common view that equates the pastor's ministry primarily with hands-on pastoral care originated. I believe that it comes from at least two sources: the biblical use of shepherd imagery and tradition. While Scripture uses shepherd imagery, shepherds did much more than just provide pastoral care for their sheep. The passages noted above demonstrate this, and so does any good book on biblical customs. Consequently this view is a misunderstanding of what shepherds did in biblical times. It assumes that a shepherd spent most of his day taking care of sheep. It would be more accurate when we hear the term *shepherd* to think of him as a sheep-leader than a sheep caregiver.

An examination of church history reveals that in various historical periods, the church emphasized different roles for the pastor. During the Reformation, the Reformers emphasized the teaching of God's Word. In the 1600s the Puritans specifically stressed the role of pastor as a "physician of the soul." They believed that the pastor's primary role was that of the shepherd of souls. Much of the emphasis today on the pastor as caregiver comes from this emphasis. While tradition helps us understand how the church has viewed the role of the pastor over the ages, we must draw our understanding from

Scripture. If tradition contradicts the Bible, it's imperative that we follow the latter over the former.

This view of pastoral ministry is wrong if the pastor of a church pours most of his time into pastoral care and little, if any, into other areas, such as communicating and encouraging the church to pursue Jesus's mission for the church—the Great Commission. It is also wrong if people insist that the primary role of all pastors must be the pastoral care of the flock.

My purpose in writing this appendix isn't to diminish the importance of pastoral care but to put it in proper biblical perspective. At a time when pastoring a church is a leadership-intensive enterprise (Peter Drucker argues that leading a large church is one of the three most difficult professions in our culture), pastors must know what their biblical role is. I am convinced that the primary role is that of leader of the flock, who at times provides pastoral care for the flock.

Appendix B

What Did Jesus Mean in Matthew 28:19–20 When He Commanded His Church to Make Disciples?

Perhaps the most important questions that a church and its leadership can ask are: What does God want us to do? What is our mandate or mission? What are our marching orders? The answer to all three questions isn't hard to find. More than two thousand years ago, the Savior predetermined the church's mission—it's the Great Commission, as found in such texts as Mark 16:15; Luke 24:46–49; John 20:21; and Matthew 28:19–20, where he says, "Make disciples." This commission raises several important questions, such as what is a disciple and what does it mean to make disciples?

If you asked ten different people in the church (including the pastoral staff) what a disciple is, you might get ten different answers. The same is true at a seminary. If the church is not clear on what Jesus meant, then it will be difficult for it to comply with his expressed will. For the church to understand what the Savior meant in Matthew 28:19–20, we must examine the main verb and its object "make disciples" and then the two participles that follow—"baptizing" and "teaching." What does all this mean?

"Make Disciples"

First, let's examine the main verb and its object: "make disciples." A common view is that a disciple is a committed believer. Thus a disciple is a believer, but a believer isn't necessarily a disciple. However, that's not how the New Testament uses this term. I contend that the normative use of the term *disciple* (though there are some obvious exceptions[1]) is of one who is a convert to or a believer in Jesus Christ. Thus the Bible teaches that a disciple isn't necessarily a Christian who has made a deeper commitment to the Savior but simply a Christian. Committed Christians are committed disciples. Uncommitted Christians are uncommitted disciples. This is clearly how Luke uses the term *disciple* in the book of Acts and his Gospel. It is evident in passages such as the following: Acts 6:1–2, 7; 9:1, 26; 11:26; 14:21–22; 15:10; 18:23; 19:9. For example, Acts 6:7 tells us that God's Word kept spreading and the number of disciples continued to increase greatly in Jerusalem. Luke isn't telling us that the number of deeply committed believers was significantly increasing. He's telling his readers that the church was making numerous converts to the faith. In Acts 9:1 Luke writes that Saul (Paul) was "breathing out murderous threats against the Lord's disciples." It's most doubtful that Saul was threatening only the mature believers. He was persecuting as many believers as he could locate. A great example is Acts 14:21 where Luke says they "won a large number of disciples" in connection with evangelism. Here they preached the gospel and won or made a large number of disciples or converts, not mature or even growing Christians. (Note that the words "won a large number of disciples" is the one Greek word *mathateusantes*, the same word as in Matthew 28:19!) Disciples, then, were synonymous with believers. Virtually all scholars acknowledge this to be the case in Acts.

So is the command "make disciples" in Matthew 28:19 to be equated with evangelism? Before we can answer this question, we must also examine a second context. The first had to do with the use of the term *disciple* in the New Testament; the second has to do with the other Great Commission passages: Mark 16:15 and Luke 24:46–49 (with Acts 1:8). In Mark 16:15 Jesus commands the disciples, "Go into all the world and preach the good news to all creation." Here "preach" like "make disciples" is the main verb (an aorist imperative) preceded by another circumstantial participle of attendant circumstance translated "go." This is clearly a proactive command to do evangelism.

In Luke 24:46–48 we have much the same message with the gospel defined: "This is what is written: The Christ will suffer and rise from the dead on the third day, and repentance and forgiveness of sins will be preached in his name to all nations, beginning at Jerusalem. You are witnesses of these things." Jesus presents the gospel message and the necessity that his witnesses preach that gospel to all nations. In these two Great Commission passages, the emphasis is clearly on evangelism and missions.

Finally, John gives us the least information in his statement of the commission. In John 20:21–22 Jesus tells the disciples that he's sending them and provides them with the Holy Spirit in anticipation of Pentecost.

We must not stop here. There's a third context. Much of Jesus's teaching of the Twelve (who are believers, except for Judas) concerns discipleship or the need for the disciple to grow in Christ (Matt. 16:24–26; 20:26–28; Luke 9:23–25). For example, Matthew 16:24 says, "Then Jesus said to his disciples, 'If anyone would come after me, he must deny himself and take up his cross and follow me.'"

So how does this relate to the passages in Acts and the other commission passages in the Gospels? The answer is that the Great Commission has both an evangelism and an edification or spiritual growth component. To make a disciple, first one has to win a person (a nondisciple) to Christ. At that point he or she becomes a disciple. It doesn't stop there. Now this new disciple needs to grow or mature as a disciple, hence the edification component.

"Baptizing and Teaching"

Having studied the main verb and its object, "make disciples," we need to examine the two participles in Matthew 28:20—"baptizing" and "teaching." The interpretation of these will address whether "make disciples" involves both evangelism and edification. While there are two feasible interpretive options, the better one is that they are circumstantial (adverbial) participles of means.[2] The NIV has taken this interpretation: "Therefore go and *make disciples* of all nations, *baptizing* them in the name of the Father and of the Son and of the Holy Spirit, and *teaching* them to obey everything I have commanded you." Dan Wallace, a Greek scholar and professor of New Testament at Dallas Seminary, writes: "Finally, the other two participles *(baptizontes, didaskontes)* should not be taken as attendant circumstance. First, they do not fit the normal pattern for attendant circumstance participles (they are present tense and follow the main verb). And second, they obviously make good sense as participles of means; i.e., the *means* by which the disciples were to make disciples was to baptize and then to teach."[3] If this is the case, then the two participles provide us with the means or the *how* for growing the new disciples. The way the church makes disciples is by baptizing and teaching its people.

But what is the significance of baptism in the life of a new disciple (believer)? Baptism is mentioned eleven times in Acts (Acts 2:38; 8:12, 16, 36, 38; 9:18; 10:48; 16:15, 33; 19:5; 22:16). In every passage except one (19:5) it's used in close association with evangelism and immediately follows someone's conversion to Christ. Baptism was the public means or activity that identified the new disciple with Jesus.[4] Baptism was serious business, as it could mean rejection by one's parents and family, even resulting in the loss of one's life.

As we have seen, it both implies or is closely associated with evangelism and was a public confession that one had become a disciple of Jesus. Thus Matthew includes evangelism in the context of disciple making.

And finally, what is the significance of *teaching*? Luke also addresses teaching in Acts (Acts 2:42; 5:25, 28; 15:35; 18:11; 28:31). Michael Wilkins summarizes this best when he says that "'teaching' introduces the activities by which the new disciple grows in discipleship."[5] The object of our teaching is obedience to Jesus's teaching. The emphasis on teaching isn't simply for the sake of knowledge. Effective teaching results in a transformed life or a maturing disciple/believer.

The Conclusion

The conclusion from the evidence above is that the two participles are best treated and translated as circumstantial participles of means. The term *make disciples (mathateusante)* is a clear reference to both evangelism (baptizing) and maturation (teaching). (Note again the use of *mathateusantes* in Acts 14:21 in the context of evangelism.) Mark and Luke emphasize the evangelism aspect of the Great Commission (and John the sending out of the disciples). Matthew emphasizes both evangelism and the need to grow disciples in their newfound faith, as he adds the need not only to baptize but to teach these new believers as well. According to other passages in the New Testament, the latter would lead the new converts to spiritual maturity (1 Cor. 3:1–4; Heb. 5:11–6:3). Therefore, the goal is for them to become mature disciples in time. This would result from a combination of being taught and obeying Jesus's commandments.

Jesus was clear about his intentions for his church. It wasn't just to teach or preach the Word, as important as those activities are. Nor was it evangelism alone, although the latter is emphasized as much as teaching. He expects his entire church (not simply a few passionate disciple makers) to move people from prebirth (unbelief) to the new birth (belief) and then to maturity. In fact, this is so important that we can measure a church's spiritual health and its ultimate success by its obedience to the Great Commission. It is fair to ask of every church's ministry how many people have become disciples (believers) and how many of these disciples are growing toward maturity. In short, it's imperative that every church make and mature disciples at home and abroad!

Note: I highly recommend Michael J. Wilkins's *Following the Master: A Biblical Theology of Discipleship* (Zondervan, 1992). Wilkins is professor of New Testament language and literature and dean of the faculty at the Talbot School of Theology, Biola University.

APPENDIX C
SAMPLE MATURITY MATRIX

I have provided this Maturity Matrix for you to use as you critique and design your disciple-making process. You have permission to make copies of this page for yourself or your planning team.

Maturity Matrix

Characteristics of Maturity

Primary Ministries

Appendix D
Survey Questions

Quantitative Survey Questions

The questions that follow are sample quantitative questions to use with your congregation as a whole. You may want to include space after each question to allow people to add comments. You would benefit by putting them on your church's website.

1. Do I invite others to the services?
   A. Strongly agree
   B. Agree
   C. Disagree
   D. Strongly disagree

2. Does the church have a clear statement of mission (direction)?
   A. Strongly agree
   B. Agree
   C. Disagree
   D. Strongly disagree

3. Can I state the church's mission (direction)?
   A. Strongly agree
   B. Agree

C. Disagree

D. Strongly disagree

4. As a church, are we accomplishing our mission well?

A. Strongly agree

B. Agree

C. Disagree

D. Strongly disagree

5. Is the church very clear about what we think God wants to accomplish through us over the next five to ten years?

A. Strongly agree

B. Agree

C. Disagree

D. Strongly disagree

6. When I think about the church's future five to ten years from now, does a clear, exciting picture come to mind?

A. Strongly agree

B. Agree

C. Disagree

D. Strongly disagree

7. Am I satisfied with the church's role in my spiritual development?

A. Strongly agree

B. Agree

C. Disagree

D. Strongly disagree

8. Does the church have a clear strategy for growing and maturing its believers?

A. Strongly agree

B. Agree

C. Disagree

D. Strongly disagree

9. Do I believe that the church is primarily responsible for my spiritual growth and development?

A. Strongly agree

B. Agree

C. Disagree

D. Strongly disagree

10. Do I believe that I need to take responsibility for my spiritual growth and development?
    A. Strongly agree
    B. Agree
    C. Disagree
    D. Strongly disagree

11. Do I regularly share my faith with lost people?
    A. Strongly agree
    B. Agree
    C. Disagree
    D. Strongly disagree

12. Does the church seem to be prospering financially?
    A. Strongly agree
    B. Agree
    C. Disagree
    D. Strongly disagree

13. Is the church experiencing numerical growth?
    A. Strongly agree
    B. Agree
    C. Disagree
    D. Strongly disagree

14. Are the facilities more than adequate for accomplishing our ministry?
    A. Strongly agree
    B. Agree
    C. Disagree
    D. Strongly disagree

15. Is the pastor an inspiring, visionary leader?
    A. Strongly agree
    B. Agree
    C. Disagree
    D. Strongly disagree

16. Is the pastor a good preacher?
    A. Strongly agree
    B. Agree
    C. Disagree
    D. Strongly disagree

17. Does the church have a strong, competent ministry staff team?
    A. Strongly agree
    B. Agree
    C. Disagree
    D. Strongly disagree

18. Is the church's worship vibrant and uplifting?
    A. Strongly agree
    B. Agree
    C. Disagree
    D. Strongly disagree

19. Does the church have a strong small-group ministry?
    A. Strongly agree
    B. Agree
    C. Disagree
    D. Strongly disagree

20. Are a small number of people doing much of the church's ministry?
    A. Strongly agree
    B. Agree
    C. Disagree
    D. Strongly disagree

21. Does the church invite constructive feedback that leads to necessary changes?
    A. Strongly agree
    B. Agree
    C. Disagree
    D. Strongly disagree

22. Is the church well aware of who lives in its geographical community?
    A. Strongly agree
    B. Agree
    C. Disagree
    D. Strongly disagree

23. Is the church aware of the pressing needs of its community?
    A. Strongly agree
    B. Agree
    C. Disagree
    D. Strongly disagree

24. Does the church minister regularly in and to its community?
 A. Strongly agree
 B. Agree
 C. Disagree
 D. Strongly disagree

Qualitative Questions

The following qualitative questions are ones that you and several others might ask of various individuals in your congregation. You may want to focus on certain ones, asking follow-up questions. For example, you might want to ask a congregant if he or she invites others to the church's services and follow it up with another question such as, Why? or Why not?

1. How long have you attended this church?
2. Where do you live?
3. How far do you drive to get to church?
4. Why do you attend this church?
5. Do you invite others to the services?
6. What is the one thing we do best?
7. Why do people come to this church?
8. What are some of the church's greatest strengths?
9. Why do people leave this church?
10. What are some of the church's greatest weaknesses?
11. Does the church have a clear statement of mission (direction)?
12. What is the church's mission (direction)?
13. As a church, how well are we accomplishing our mission?
14. What do you think God wants to accomplish through our church over the next five to ten years?
15. What picture comes to mind when you think about the church five or ten years from now? Does it excite you?
16. What church programs and/or activities are you involved in?
17. Are you satisfied with the church's role in your spiritual development?
18. Does the church have a clear strategy for growing and maturing its believers? If so, can you articulate it?
19. What could the church do differently to help you grow spiritually?
20. Is the church responsible for your spiritual growth and development?
21. Do you need to take responsibility for your spiritual growth and development?
22. Do you regularly share your faith with lost people?
23. Is the church prospering financially?
24. Is the church experiencing numerical growth?

25. Are the facilities adequate and kept in good repair?
26. Is the pastor an inspiring, visionary leader?
27. Is the pastor a good preacher?
28. Does the church have a strong, competent ministry staff team?
29. Is the church's worship vibrant and uplifting?
30. Does the church have a strong small-group ministry?
31. Are a small number of people doing much of the church's ministry?
32. Does the church invite constructive feedback and make necessary changes?
33. Who lives in the church's geographical community?
34. What are some pressing needs of our community?
35. Is the church involved in ministry in and to its community?

APPENDIX E

CHARACTER ASSESSMENTS

Men's Character Assessment for Ministry

Over the years, leaders have discovered that godly character is critical to effective ministry for Christ. However, no one is perfect, and all of us have our weaknesses and flaws as well as strengths. This character assessment is to help you determine your character strengths and weaknesses so that you can know where you are strong and where you need to develop and grow. The characteristics are found in 1 Timothy 3:1–7 and Titus 1:6–9.

Directions: Circle the number that best represents how you would rate yourself in each area.

1. I am "above reproach." I have a good reputation among people in general. I have done nothing that someone could use as an accusation against me.

   Weak   1   2   3   4   5   6   7   8   Strong

2. I am the "husband of one wife." If married, not only do I have only one wife but I am not physically or mentally promiscuous, for I am focused only on her.

   Weak   1   2   3   4   5   6   7   8   Strong

3. I am "temperate." I am a well-balanced person. I do not overdo my use of alcohol, etc. I am not excessive in any behavior or given to extremes in beliefs, etc.

Weak   1   2   3   4   5   6   7   8   Strong

4. I am "sensible." I show good judgment in life and have a proper (humble) perspective regarding myself and my abilities.

Weak   1   2   3   4   5   6   7   8   Strong

5. I am "respectable." I conduct my life in an honorable way, and people have and show respect for me.

Weak   1   2   3   4   5   6   7   8   Strong

6. I am "hospitable." I use my residence as a place to serve and minister to Christians and non-Christians alike.

Weak   1   2   3   4   5   6   7   8   Strong

7. I am "able to teach." When I teach the Bible, I show an aptitude for handling the Scriptures with reasonable skill.

Weak   1   2   3   4   5   6   7   8   Strong

8. I am "not given to drunkenness." If I drink alcoholic beverages or indulge in other acceptable but potentially addictive practices, I do so in moderation.

Weak   1   2   3   4   5   6   7   8   Strong

9. I am "not violent." I am under control. I do not lose control to the point that I strike or cause damage to other people or their property.

Weak   1   2   3   4   5   6   7   8   Strong

10. I am "gentle." I am a kind, meek (not weak), forbearing person who does not insist on his rights or resort to violence.

Weak   1   2   3   4   5   6   7   8   Strong

11. I am "not quarrelsome." I am an uncontentious peacemaker who avoids hostile situations with people.

Weak   1   2   3   4   5   6   7   8   Strong

12. I am "not a lover of money." Making money is not a top priority for me. I seek first his righteousness, knowing that God will supply my needs.

Weak   1   2   3   4   5   6   7   8   Strong

13. I "manage my family well." If I am married and have a family, my children are believers who obey me with respect. People do not think of or accuse them of being wild or disobedient.

Weak   1   2   3   4   5   6   7   8   Strong

14. I am "not a recent convert." I am not a new Christian, and I do not struggle constantly with pride and conceit.

Weak   1   2   3   4   5   6   7   8   Strong

15. I have "a good reputation with outsiders." Though lost people may not agree with my religious convictions, they still respect me as a person.

Weak   1   2   3   4   5   6   7   8   Strong

16. I am "not overbearing." I am not self-willed, stubborn, or arrogant.

Weak   1   2   3   4   5   6   7   8   Strong

17. I am "not quick-tempered." I am not inclined toward anger (an angry person), and I do not lose my temper quickly and easily.

Weak   1   2   3   4   5   6   7   8   Strong

18. I am "not pursuing dishonest gain." I am not fond of or involved in any wrongful practices that result in fraudulent gain.

Weak   1   2   3   4   5   6   7   8   Strong

19. I "love what is good." I love the things that honor God.

Weak   1   2   3   4   5   6   7   8   Strong

20. I am "upright." I live in accordance with the laws of God and man.

Weak   1   2   3   4   5   6   7   8   Strong

21. I am "holy." I am a devout person whose life is generally pleasing to God.

Weak   1   2   3   4   5   6   7   8   Strong

22. I "hold firmly to the faith." I understand, hold to, and attempt to guard God's truth. I also encourage others, while refuting those who oppose the truth.

Weak   1   2   3   4   5   6   7   8   **Strong**

When you have completed this character assessment, note those characteristics that you gave the lowest rating (a 4 or below). You should develop the character goals to which you gave the lowest rating, focusing on one or two at a time.

Women's Character Assessment for Ministry

Over the years, leaders have discovered that godly character is critical to effective ministry for Christ. However, no one is perfect, and all of us have our weaknesses and flaws as well as strengths. This character assessment is to help you determine your character strengths and weaknesses so that you can know where you are strong and where you need to develop and grow. The characteristics are found in 1 Timothy 2:9–10; 3:11; Titus 2:3–5; and 1 Peter 3:1–4.

Directions: Circle the number that best represents how you would rate yourself in each area.

1. I am "worthy of respect." I find that most people who know me respect me and tend to honor me as a dignified person who is serious about spiritual things.

   Weak   1   2   3   4   5   6   7   8   Strong

2. I am not a "malicious talker." I do not slander people, whether believers or unbelievers.

   Weak   1   2   3   4   5   6   7   8   Strong

3. I am "temperate." I am a well-balanced person. I do not overdo my use of alcohol, etc. I am not excessive in my behavior or given to extremes in beliefs, etc.

   Weak   1   2   3   4   5   6   7   8   Strong

4. I am "trustworthy in everything." The Lord and people find me to be a faithful person in everything.

   Weak   1   2   3   4   5   6   7   8   Strong

5. I live "reverently." I have a deep respect for God and live in awe of him.

   Weak   1   2   3   4   5   6   7   8   Strong

6. I am "not addicted to much wine." If I drink alcoholic beverages, I do so in moderation. I am not addicted to them.

   Weak   1   2   3   4   5   6   7   8   Strong

7. I teach "what is good." I share with other women what God has taught me from his Word and from life in general.

   Weak   1   2   3   4   5   6   7   8   Strong

8. I "love my husband." If I am married, I love my husband according to 1 Corinthians 13:4–8.

Weak   1   2   3   4   5   6   7   8   Strong

9. I "love my children." If I am married and have children, I love my children.

Weak   1   2   3   4   5   6   7   8   Strong

10. I am "self-controlled." I do not let other people or things run my life, and I am not a person of extremes or excessive behavior.

Weak   1   2   3   4   5   6   7   8   Strong

11. I am "pure." I am not involved emotionally or physically in sexual immorality.

Weak   1   2   3   4   5   6   7   8   Strong

12. I am "busy at home." If I am a married person, then I take care of my responsibilities at home.

Weak   1   2   3   4   5   6   7   8   Strong

13. I am "kind." I am essentially a good person.

Weak   1   2   3   4   5   6   7   8   Strong

14. I am "subject to my husband." If I am married, I let my husband take responsibility for and lead our marriage, and I follow his leadership.

Weak   1   2   3   4   5   6   7   8   Strong

15. I have "a gentle and quiet spirit." I am a mild, easygoing person who wins others over by a pure and reverent life more than by my words.

Weak   1   2   3   4   5   6   7   8   Strong

16. I "dress modestly." I wear clothing that is decent and shows propriety.

Weak   1   2   3   4   5   6   7   8   Strong

17. I "do good deeds." I do those things that are appropriate for women who profess to know and worship God.

Weak   1   2   3   4   5   6   7   8   Strong

When you have completed this character assessment, note those characteristics that you gave the lowest rating (a 4 or below). You should develop the character goals to which you gave the lowest rating, focusing on one or two at a time.

APPENDIX F

MINISTRY DESCRIPTION

Job Title: Christian Education Director with a focus on Children's Ministries

Job Profile: Ideally the Christian Education Director has gifts or abilities in the following areas: leadership, discernment, shepherding, administration, encouragement, and teaching.

The director needs a passion for adults as well as kids (works primarily with adults on behalf of the kids). A primary function will be the ability to work with and develop adults and teens as leaders.

This person's ideal temperament is a D/I on the *Personal Profile*.

The director needs to see life "through the eyes of a child." This person should be in touch with children—their world and culture.

Finally, the director should be a visionary who can take the children's ministry to the next level in its development.

Job Summary: The director is responsible for the children's Sunday school program (nursery through youth), children's church, the annual vacation Bible school, and the Sunday school and worship nurseries. However, the director will focus primarily on children's ministries.

Duties:
 A. Sunday School
  1. Recruit teachers and floaters.
  2. Train teachers and floaters.

3. Evaluate teachers and floaters.
4. Encourage teachers and floaters.
5. Assist teachers and monitor Sunday morning program.
6. Maintain supplies and facilities.
7. Select and approve all curriculum.
8. Plan and make preparation for class expansion.
9. Maintain a substitute teacher list.

B. Children's Church
   1. Presentation of church program.
   2. Recruit workers for leadership.
   3. Train workers for leadership.
   4. Select the curriculum.

C. Vacation Bible School
   1. Recruit a director and other leaders.
   2. Choose curriculum and coordinate other materials.
   3. Recruit teachers and workers.

D. Sunday School and Worship Service Nurseries
   1. Recruit directors.
   2. Help recruit people as workers.

E. Miscellaneous
   1. Develop the core values, mission, vision, and strategy for the Christian education program.
   2. Attend board meetings.
   3. Attend staff meetings.
   4. Conduct personal background checks.
   5. Conduct personal reference checks.
   6. Preach as needed.

Reports to: Senior Pastor

Works with: Elder responsible for Christian education

APPENDIX G

RELATIONAL SKILLS INVENTORY

The following are some critical people skill sets for leaders in general and pastors in particular. Rate your ability in each skill by placing a check in the appropriate box.

Skills	strong	above average	below average	weak	don't know
Listening	☐	☐	☐	☐	☐
Networking	☐	☐	☐	☐	☐
Conflict resolution	☐	☐	☐	☐	☐
Decision making	☐	☐	☐	☐	☐
Risk taking	☐	☐	☐	☐	☐
Problem solving	☐	☐	☐	☐	☐
Confronting	☐	☐	☐	☐	☐
Encouraging	☐	☐	☐	☐	☐
Trust building	☐	☐	☐	☐	☐
Inspiring/Motivating	☐	☐	☐	☐	☐
Team building	☐	☐	☐	☐	☐
Consensus building	☐	☐	☐	☐	☐
Recruiting	☐	☐	☐	☐	☐
Hiring and firing	☐	☐	☐	☐	☐
Conducting meetings	☐	☐	☐	☐	☐
Recognizing and rewarding	☐	☐	☐	☐	☐

Skills	strong	above average	below average	weak	don't know
Questioning	☐	☐	☐	☐	☐
Disagreeing	☐	☐	☐	☐	☐
Confronting	☐	☐	☐	☐	☐
Counseling	☐	☐	☐	☐	☐
Mentoring	☐	☐	☐	☐	☐
Community building	☐	☐	☐	☐	☐
Challenging	☐	☐	☐	☐	☐
Trusting	☐	☐	☐	☐	☐
Empowering	☐	☐	☐	☐	☐
Evaluating	☐	☐	☐	☐	☐
Managing/Administering	☐	☐	☐	☐	☐
Leading	☐	☐	☐	☐	☐
Delegating	☐	☐	☐	☐	☐
Disciplining	☐	☐	☐	☐	☐
Evangelizing	☐	☐	☐	☐	☐
Correcting	☐	☐	☐	☐	☐

Appendix H

TASK SKILLS INVENTORY

The following are some critical task skill sets for leaders in general and pastors in particular. Rate your ability in each skill by placing a check in the appropriate box.

Skills	strong	above average	below average	weak	don't know
Teaching	☐	☐	☐	☐	☐
Researching	☐	☐	☐	☐	☐
Values discovery	☐	☐	☐	☐	☐
Communicating	☐	☐	☐	☐	☐
Mission development	☐	☐	☐	☐	☐
Mission casting	☐	☐	☐	☐	☐
Vision development	☐	☐	☐	☐	☐
Vision casting	☐	☐	☐	☐	☐
Strategizing	☐	☐	☐	☐	☐
Reflecting	☐	☐	☐	☐	☐
Time management	☐	☐	☐	☐	☐
Stress management	☐	☐	☐	☐	☐
Use of technology	☐	☐	☐	☐	☐
Prioritizing	☐	☐	☐	☐	☐
Writing	☐	☐	☐	☐	☐
General planning	☐	☐	☐	☐	☐

Skills	strong	above average	below average	weak	don't know
Strategic planning	☐	☐	☐	☐	☐
Making presentations	☐	☐	☐	☐	☐
Monitoring	☐	☐	☐	☐	☐
Praying	☐	☐	☐	☐	☐
Creating/Creativity	☐	☐	☐	☐	☐
Implementing	☐	☐	☐	☐	☐
Organizing	☐	☐	☐	☐	☐
Budgeting	☐	☐	☐	☐	☐
Advertising	☐	☐	☐	☐	☐

Notes

Introduction

1. Aubrey Malphurs, *Advanced Strategic Planning: A New Model for Church and Ministry Leaders,* 2nd ed. (Grand Rapids: Baker, 2005).

Chapter 2 How Are We Doing?

1. Philip Jenkins, *The Next Christendom* (New York: Oxford University Press, 2002), 2.
2. Ibid., 94.
3. Ibid.
4. Ibid., 3.
5. George Gallup Jr., *The Unchurched American—Ten Years Later* (Princeton, NJ: Princeton Religion Research Center, 1988), 2.
6. George Barna, "Unchurched People," Barna Research Online, 2005, at http://www.barna .org/FlexPage.aspx?Page=Topic&TopicID=22, 1.
7. George Barna, "One in Three Adults Is Unchurched," Barna Research Online, March 28, 2005, at http://www.barna.org/FlexPageaspx?Page=BarnaUpdate&BarnaUpdateID=185, 1.
8. George Barna, "Generational Differences," Barna Research Online, 2004, at http://www .barna.org/FlexPage.aspx?Page=Topic&TopicID=22, 1.
9. "U.S. Attendance at Services Is Down in Poll," *Dallas Morning News,* May 28, 1994, 43A.
10. Cathy L. Grossman and Anthony DeBarros, "Still One Nation under God," *USA Today,* December 24, 2001, 2D.
11. C. Kirk Hadaway, Penny L. Marler, and Mark Chaves, "What the Polls Don't Show: A Closer Look at U.S. Church Attendance," *American Sociological Review* (December 1993): 741–52.
12. David T. Olson, "29 Interesting Facts about the American Church" (2006), Facts 4–7, at http://www.theamericanchurch.org.
13. Ibid., Fact 17.
14. Bob Gilliam, "Are Most Churches Intentionally Making Disciples? Findings from the Spiritual Journey Evaluation" (unpublished paper, circulated March 29, 1995), 1.
15. Greg L. Hawkins and Cally Parkinson, *Reveal: Where Are You?* (Chicago: Willow Creek Resources, 2007), 4.
16. Dietrich Bonhoeffer, *The Cost of Discipleship* (New York: Macmillan, 1937), 64–65.

Chapter 3 What Are We Talking About?

1. Michael J. Wilkins, *Following the Master: A Biblical Theology of Discipleship* (Grand Rapids: Zondervan, 1992), 26.
2. Ibid.
3. J. Dwight Pentecost, *Design for Discipleship* (Grand Rapids: Zondervan, 1971), 14.
4. Walter A. Henrichsen, *Disciples Are Made—Not Born* (Wheaton, IL: Victor, 1974), 40.
5. Leroy Eims, *The Lost Art of Disciple Making* (Grand Rapids: Zondervan, 1978), 61.
6. Ibid., 187.
7. Charles C. Ryrie, *A Survey of Bible Doctrine* (Chicago: Moody Press, 1972), 136.
8. Wilkins, *Following the Master*, 39.
9. Ibid., 40.
10. Ibid., 221.

Chapter 4 Whose Job Is It?

1. Hawkins and Parkinson, *Reveal*, 36.
2. Wilkins, *Following the Master*, 36.
3. George Barna, "Americans Have Commitment Issues, New Survey Shows," Barna Research Online, April 18, 2006, at http://www.barna.org/FlexPage.aspx?Page=BarnaUpdate&BarnaUpdateID=235.
4. George Barna, "A Faith Revolution Is Redefining 'Church' according to New Study," Barna Research Online, October 10, 2005, at http://www.barna.org/FlexPage.aspx?Page=BarnaUpdate&BarnaUpdateID=201.
5. Hawkins and Parkinson, *Reveal*, 47.

Chapter 5 How Did Jesus Make Disciples?

1. Wilkins, *Following the Master*, 216–17.
2. Ibid., 36.

Chapter 6 How Did the Church Make Disciples?

1. Wilkins, *Following the Master*, 279.
2. Robert Banks, *Paul's Idea of Community*, rev. ed. (Peabody, MA: Hendrickson), 35.

Chapter 7 How Would We Know a Mature Disciple If We Saw One?

1. Gilliam, "Are Most Churches Intentionally Making Disciples?" 1.
2. Ibid.
3. Hawkins and Parkinson, *Reveal*, 53.
4. Ibid., 39, 42.
5. Wilkins, *Following the Master*, 277–78.
6. Ibid., 279.

Chapter 8 How Do Churches Make Mature Disciples?

1. Lynne and Bill Hybels, *Rediscovering Church* (Grand Rapids: Zondervan, 1995), 169.
2. Dan Kimball, *The Emerging Church* (Grand Rapids: Zondervan, 2003), 217.
3. Hybels, *Rediscovering Church*, 169.
4. Ibid., chapter 11.
5. Rick Warren, *The Purpose Driven Church* (Grand Rapids: Zondervan, 1995), 142.
6. Kimball, *The Emerging Church*, 224.

7. While I do not entirely agree with them, Thom Rainer and Eric Geiger's book *Simple Church* (Nashville: B&H Publishing, 2006) has influenced my thinking on this.

Chapter 9 Are You Making Disciples?

1. Hawkins and Parkinson, *Reveal*, 24.
2. Ibid., 4.
3. Ibid., 67.
4. Tom Holiday, "Evaluating Your Church on Purpose: Part 2," *Rick Warren's Ministry Toolbox* 333 (October 17, 2007), at http://www.pastors.com?RWMT/printerfriendlyt .asp?issue=333&artID=10921.

Chapter 10 How to Recruit the Right Staff

1. Peter Drucker, *Managing the Non-profit Organization* (New York: Harper Collins, 1990), 145.
2. Gary L. McIntosh, *Staff Your Church for Growth* (Grand Rapids: Baker, 2000), 43. I suspect that these are figures for a middle-class suburban church as opposed to a lower-income inner-city church. You might need to adjust the figures to match your situation. It is most likely that a lower-income inner-city church would not be able to afford a large staff and would need to recruit more laypersons for ministry.
3. Bill Hybels, *Courageous Leadership* (Grand Rapids: Zondervan, 2002), 85.
4. Larry Bossidy and Ram Charan, *Execution: The Discipline of Getting Things Done* (New York: Crown Business, 2002), 112.
5. Peter F. Drucker, "Management's New Paradigms," in *MBA in a Box*, ed. Joel Kurtzman, (New York: Crown Business, 2004), 192.
6. In the job descriptions at Northwood, a church that I pastored, we carefully spelled out all the ministry responsibilities. Consequently, we could not randomly dump new responsibilities on staff without first discussing it and their current load with them. We also discussed increased compensation for increased responsibilities.
7. Mark Hendricks, "How Many Employees Reporting Directly to You Is Too Many?" *Entrepreneur*, January 2008 at http://www.entrepreneur.com/magazine/entrepreneur/2001/ january/35688.html.

Chapter 11 How to Prepare a Strategic Budget

1. Hybels, *Courageous Leadership*, 98.
2. Ibid (italics mine).
3. Aubrey Malphurs and Steve Stroope, *Money Matters in Church: A Practical Guide for Leaders* (Grand Rapids: Baker, 2007).
4. Aubrey Malphurs, *Developing a Vision for Ministry in the Twenty-first Century*, 2nd ed. (Grand Rapids: Baker, 1999).
5. George Barna, *How to Increase Giving in Your Church* (Ventura, CA: Regal, 1997), 92–93.
6. Ibid., 118.
7. "God, Money, and the Pastor," *Leadership*, Fall 2002, 30–31.

Appendix B What Did Jesus Mean in Matthew 28:19–20 When He Commanded His Church to Make Disciples?

1. Some exceptions are the disciples of Moses (John 9:28), the disciples of the Pharisees (Matt. 22:16; Mark 2:18), the disciples of John (Mark 2:18; John 1:35), and the disciples of Jesus who left him (John 6:60–66).

2. The second option is to treat them as circumstantial (adverbial) participles of attendant circumstance. If this is correct, then the participles *baptizing* and *teaching* express an idea not subordinate to as above but coordinate to or on a par with the main verb (make disciples). You would translate the main verb and the participles as a series of coordinate verbs, the mood of which is dictated by the main verb that in this case is imperative (aorist imperative). The verse would read: "Go, therefore, and *make disciples* of all nations, *baptize* them in the name of the Father and of the Son and of the Holy Spirit, and *teach* them to obey everything that I have commanded you." A former Dallas Seminary Greek professor, Philip Williams, takes this view in "Grammar Notes on the Noun and the Verb and Certain Other Items" (unpublished class notes, which were used by Dr. Buist Fanning in his course Advanced Greek Grammar, 1977), 53–54. The conclusion here is that the passage addresses a series of separate, coordinate chronological acts or steps. The first is to go, which implies proactivity. The second is to make disciples. The third is to baptize those disciples, and the fourth is to teach them. However, I believe that Dan Wallace makes the better argument for these being circumstantial participles of means. While I don't believe that *baptizontes* and *didaskontes* are circumstantial participles of attendant circumstance, I do believe that the first participle in verse 19 *(poreuthentes)* is. It draws its mood from or is coordinate to the main verb *(mathateusate)*, which is imperative. Jesus is commanding them to make disciples and to be proactive about it.

3. Daniel B. Wallace, *Greek Grammar beyond the Basics* (Grand Rapids: Zondervan, 1996), 645.

4. See Wilkins, *Following the Master*, 189.

5. Ibid., 189–90.

SUBJECT AND NAME INDEX

Scripture Index

253
M259S

120332

THE**MALPHURS**GROUP
ENVISION TOMORROW TODAY

Aubrey Malphurs, Ph.D.

President
The Malphurs Group

Professor
Dallas Theological Seminary

Let us serve you!
We offer training and consulting services such as:

- Strategic planning
- Church refocusing
- Church planting

- Values discovery
- Personal leadership coaching

Visit our Web site! Features include:

- Books
- Seminars
- Newsletters

- Events
- Resources
- and more…

aubrey@malphursgroup.com • www.malphursgroup.com

For more info: 214.841.3777
7916 Briar Brook Court • Dallas, Texas 75218

3 4711 00198 1663